SINGLE: IN MY OWN LANE

THE ROAD TO MAXIMIZING YOUR SINGLE LIFE

T.L. HAYES

An Imprint of Hayes Media Enterprises

There are no words that can express how truly humble yet proud I am of the manifestation of this book. It was my creator, that granted me the creativity, to create this body of work. And to Him I dedicate this book, as I do my life. Thank You Father!

I dedicate this book to my heartbeats. Alayna. Peyton. Denver. You three are the reason daddy works so hard. I am working to provide for you all the example, blueprint, and inspiration that I never had. Making it clear that fathers matter. Daddy loves you!

I dedicate this book to the journey. You were long, strenuous, and many times frustrating. And I thank you. I thank you for extending me, and exposing me. Because of you I am a better author, and this book is full of power.

Finally, I dedicate this book to my love. You are the core of my being. The silver lining in my dark cloud. And the star of my sky. When I spoke to my world and said "let there be light", I was talking about YOU.

Single: Living In My Own Lane

Table of Contents:

Introduction: Getting Beyond the Myth

Chapter 1: Are You Single?

- What is singleness?
- The Foundation of Singleness

Chapter 2: Along But Not Lonely

- Who told you that?
- Study being single
- All-one
- Are you afraid to be alone?

Chapter 3: The Beast of Being Alone

- Insecurity
- Jealousy
- Bitterness
- Complication
- Dependency
- Settlement and Compromise

Chapter 4: The Beauty of Being Alone

- Me-Search
- Identified Purpose
- Venting Opportunity
- Permission to be You

- Awakening of Greatness

Chapter 5: Alone Is Designed by God

- A place I will Show You
- The Fight of a Champion
- Exclusive Revelations
- Urgency for Discovery

Chapter 6: You Can't Give Me What I Already Have

- Love Must Be Understood
- What's in Will Always Come Out
- An Addition; Not an Initiation
- Let them be Anything but "Everything"

Chapter 7: One Person Show

- Do You
- Build "Team You"
- The Gift of Selfishness
- Dinner: Party of One

Chapter 8: The Standards of Singleness

- What type of "watch" are you?
- Value Births Respect
- Standards Provide Safety
- Know the Truth, or Fall for the Lie
- I Am

Chapter 9: Image Is Everything

- Start Building
- Vision Authenticates Imagination

Chapter 10: Let's Talk About Sex

- Soul Ties

- Protect more Than Your Body
- Is It Worth It?
- It's Worth the Wait
- The Choice Not to Wait
- Waiting Is Hard

Chapter 11: Leave Me Alone

- Can You Handle Company
- Best to Remain Alone
- It Is Not Good for You to Be Alone
- Living Single

Single: In My Own Lane

T.L. Hayes

THE ROAD TO MAXIMIZING YOUR SINGLE LIFE

Introduction:

Getting Beyond the Myth

There is a terrible myth that has survived for decades which details that when you are single you are cursed. Plagued. And/or excluded from romance. The notion has been that when you are single, you're lonely. Desperate for love. Thirsty for companionship. And written off as damaged goods. It has been summed up that when you are single, you are living some sort of prison sentence. With hopes of one day making parole.

But going against the myth, there are millions of singles that will contest that they don't live under the curse of being single. They aren't lonely. And they don't view their singleness as a prison sentence. They may be single but they find it to be more of a blessing than a curse. They aren't sitting starving for company or romance. They aren't even in the field looking for a partner. These individuals value the freedom of being single.

Now the contradictive side of the myth has been that when you are single, you are living the dream.

Millions of couples around the world have become envious of single people. Mainly because they too (like the happily single) are reminded of the freedom that singleness affords and that they no longer have. They grow green with jealousy because singles have no one to answer to. No one to consult with before they make a decision. No curfews. No obligations. And best of all no commitments.

However, there are a countless number of singles that wish they didn't have so much "freedom." Somewhere their "freedom" has turned to "frustration". Yes, they are frustrated with the dating scene. Frustrated with coming home to no one. Frustrated with being in the wedding party, but never having their own. And with the clock continuing to tick they wonder if they will ever find someone to share their life with.

Whether you are *satisfied* or *suffering* in your singleness this book is for you.

This book is designed to help you maximize your life as a person *outside of a relationship*. This book is loaded with tips and tools that will help you live your best life. We will explore parts about you that you may have never taken a notice of; yet with tears in your eyes one moment, and laughter in your heart the next, you'll be glad that you finally did.

This book mixed with your honesty and openness will become the road map to helping you live life IN YOUR OWN LANE. No more comparing yourself to other people. No more complaining about your flaws. No more wishing you had someone to come along and make you happy. No more discounting your time and attention; and dumbing down your standards just to have someone around.

If you are in a relationship and looking to bring more value and substance to your union, this book is for you too!

This book is more than an aide for the single looking to find real love. This book is for the individual that is tired of *life as usual*. This book is for the individual that refuses to settle as a copycat, or duplicate of someone else. The wisdom inside each chapter will transform you, motivate you, and place you directly on the road of wholeness, security, and happiness.

This book will change the way you view partnership and relationships entirely. Broadening your idea of what it truly means to bring something to the table.

If you are ready to live life better, fuller, and in your own way…Let's begin!

Chapter 1

ARE YOU SINGLE?

I know you probably thinking, "of course, I am single; that's one of the main reasons for purchasing this book." I hear you, but again I ask you the question... Are you single? Now, at this point you're like "don't remind me". Why? Because Singleness has become a term you know all too well. You have been single for so long that you have become a scholar on the subject. You are so skilled at being single you don't even remember what it feels like to be in a relationship. You can't recall your last date. In fact, you don't even know the last time the offer even came up. So, when I question your singleness, I am sure, you sarcastically laugh and answer my question with a question of your own that says "what else is new?"

Sure, for some of you it is by choice. You don't have time for the dramas. The emotional drama. The arguing drama. The cheating drama. The baby mama/ baby daddy drama. Heck, if you wanted drama you would have went to acting school. I hear you loud and clear.

But for some of you, singleness isn't a choice. And while you don't want any drama either, you would like something to spice things up. You would love a man to hold you. A woman to encourage you. Someone to spend time with. Someone to laugh and share your day with. Someone to compliment how beautiful you are. Someone to applaud your accomplishments. I know you're tired of being a bridesmaid, and you're ready to finally put on your own "white dress", walk down the aisle, and marry the man of your dreams. And I am sure while you are building the life you've always wanted, it will all be nothing without a beautiful woman to share it with. I hear you as well.

Then, there are some that will welcome it all. They're like "give me the man." "Give me the woman." "I don't care if they have baby mama/ baby daddy drama." "I don't care if we argue." "I don't mind going on the emotional rollercoaster." These are those that are called "ride or die". These are those that are referred to as "down". Meaning they are down to ride come whatever turbulence. They are so committed to being in a relationship that they will pull up their sleeves and take on any and all opposition. With hopes of having someone to cuddle up next too at night. Even if this means the person they are pursuing is married. Even if that person is gone first thing in the morning. Even if they are more bad than they are good to them. They are just in love with the idea of having someone around. For after all anything is better than the cold reality of singleness. The lonely reality of desiring love, with no one to make the exchange.

No matter what side you find yourself, it all falls under the category of being single. Or does it?

Please allow me a moment to give you a different thought to consider. What if I told you that you aren't single at all? What if

I told you that your lack of a ring, lack of a spouse, and lack of wedding vows didn't automatically constitute you as being single? What if I told you that singleness is a state of being, rather than a relational status? Some of you would deny my theory. While the rest of you hunger for an explanation. I am glad I have your attention. Now allow me to give you revelation.

What is Singleness?

Now to answer my initial question accurately, you would have to know what singleness is. For how can you identify yourself as something you have no reference, or real knowledge? For so long we are taught and we conclude that singleness is to be without a spouse. Not married. And while you are not incorrect, you are incomplete. Please, don't feel embarrassed, you are not the only one that has drawn this conclusion. I, like millions of people, have defined singleness this very same way. And because of it we have countless people identifying themselves as single when they really are not. Everyone that is absent of a ring or spouse, is not single. They are simply unmarried. I hear some wise person questioning "well aren't those the same thing?" Well, after this proposal you'll find that the two couldn't be more different.

A person that is unmarried is just like it sounds, not married. "Unmarried" is a relational status. While it's antithesis, "single", is a state of being. For you could very well be unmarried, and be far from single. No, I am not suggesting friends with benefits. Nor am I considering the casual dating. I am referring solely to the state of being of the individual in question. Singleness is the state of being whole. Singleness is to be separate. Singleness means unique. Singleness means independent. Singleness means fully sufficient.

So, you see it could be that you are not single at all. It could be that you are just unmarried. But the big question now becomes "which one are you?"

It is on this canvas that I wanted to paint the portrait of singleness. For there are so many unmarried men and women, as well as married men and women that have no concrete understanding of what it means to truly be single. And throughout this book I intend to shine light on what it means to be single and how to fully maximize in the state of singleness.

The foundation of Singleness

It is imperative that we understand what singleness is because singleness is the foundation of every relationship. Whether it be amongst friends, colleagues, business partners, relatives, or romantic partners, singleness is necessary. Singleness is what makes partnership work. And the failure of any partnership is not for any reason other than that fact that one or both parties lacked the state of being single. Remember single is a state of wholeness. Separation. Independence. Completion. Full sufficiency.

Wholeness:

When a person lacks being whole, they look outwardly for something or someone to fill the empty space(s). They never can provide 100% of themselves to anything, or anyone because they lack the state of being whole. A partial person, can never give you a full commitment. And for this reason, the person is unreliable. Non-dependable. And here today gone tomorrow. So, anyone that befriends them, partners with them, or enters a relationship with them is bound for disappointment.

This is why the last guy you dated couldn't give you all his attention. This is why the last woman you were involved with only gave you part of her, and the remaining was devoted to another. It wasn't that he/she was evil, immoral, or devious, they simply lacked wholeness. And when a person lacks wholeness, they can't pretend they do. Eventually the lack thereof will be revealed. And when it does someone usually ends up hurt.

When the state of wholeness is missing, it leaves vacancy for half. Half-truths. Half-apologizes. Half-commitments. Half-effort. Half-sincerity. Half-affection. Half-of them. This is how commitment anxiety is developed. This is why one can't fully give themselves to another. This is why a person can't fully trust another. It is not because they were hurt. It is not because they were cheated on. These are all qualifying variables, but the root issue here is lack of wholeness. They depended on another to complete them and make them whole, but they never considered the truth that no one has the power to make another whole. You are not a half looking for our other half. You are a whole person, worthy of meeting and developing relationship with another whole person.

LANE CHANGE: You are not whole the moment you find a significate other, you are whole once you find the significance of yourself.

Separate:

To be separate is powerful. **To be separate is having the ability to stand in solitary**. When you master being separate, you relinquish the need to have someone around. The most powerful partnership, or relationship is when both people are great separately. A song writer said "I am movement by myself, but I am a force when we are together". What he meant is "I am good alone, but I am better with you." This is where the term "power couple" comes in. The man is powerful in his own lane, and so is the woman in hers, but when the two worlds collide, they become epic.

It should never take for someone to come along before you realize your greatness. They shouldn't be the activation of your greatness, but they should be an addition to your greatness. We will discuss this more later. However, before you can form a power couple, both must first be powerful individuals. Before they can be a loving couple, the two must be loving individuals. Before they can be a reliable couple, the two must be...well I think you get the picture.

Independent:

Independence is often confused with being separate; but like singleness and unmarried, the two are very different. Being

Separate is the ability and willingness to stand alone. While independence is having the wherewithal of not having to rely on another. There is nothing worse than to be in a partnership, or relationship with someone that can't uphold there end of the load. When you are independent, you become accustom to carrying your own load. You don't look for handouts, neither do you sulk in pity parties for not having help. You put on your armor and you go to work.

You carry the load of the single mom/dad. You pay the bills. You cook the meals. You wash the clothes. You make it happen with or without acknowledgment. For you are not doing this to be applauded, you are doing this because it has to be done. And the last thing you have time for is begging someone to come and help you carry the weight.

When you are independent you aren't needy. You don't need to have anyone around to have a great time. You don't need a compliment to feel pretty. You don't need the validation that you're a great guy. While all of these are wonderful, and would be nice, they don't make or break you, because you've reminded yourself of this already.

Independence is more than not needing someone to pick up the tab, or cover the rent. Independence is the beauty of not needing another to confirm the truth about you that you already know. Independence means you are humble enough to take a compliment, but confident enough to not thirst for it.

So how independent are you?

Complete:

The state of being complete, compliments the state of wholeness. For when you are complete, you don't consider yourself half. What does this mean? I am glad you asked. I often counsel singles and they say things like "I want to feel whole" "I need someone to complete me", or "I think I have found my better half", but every time I hear these statements, or any variation, I pose the question "who told you that you were half?"

This is a hole that many unmarried people fall into. They think that they need someone else to come along and complete them. They have this silly idea that they aren't whole or complete until they have a partner or spouse to come along and balance them out. But the truth is no one can ever come and bring you what you think is missing. If you were half when the two of you linked up, you will be half after the two of you are together. And who wants a half partner? How unfair is that? Right now, this may be stinging someone reading, but let me ease the pain by informing you that you are complete with or without a partner.

And if you don't feel complete, you must find your wholeness and complete state of being from God, and not another person. When you are not complete, there is nothing another person can add to you but trouble. The state of feeling incomplete puts you in a dangerous place, because you'll do anything out of a desperate need to feel complete. And there are many men/women that prey on the incomplete. They use them. Abuse them. And leave them even worse than when they met them.

When you are misled to believe you are incomplete, you'll often fill that void with anything or anyone just to relieve the emptiness. This is why people stay with cheaters, dead beats, and even married individuals, because they are trying to fill a space. Sure, they know it is not right, but they just want to fill the void, even if it cost them their morals, values, and dignity.

Full Sufficiency:

This is the complete opposite of feeling incomplete. Full sufficiency is the state of wholeness, separation, independence, and completion all wrapped into one. When you are fully sufficient you are the total package. This is the essence of singleness. When you are fully sufficient you have arrived to the pinnacle of singleness. For when you are fully sufficient, you have met the pre-requisite of being in a partnership or relationship. When you are fully sufficient you've become relationship material. Many say they are "wifey material" or "hubby material", but until you are fully sufficient, you have no idea. When you have reached this state, you don't "need" a relationship, but you can now appreciate, and handle being in one. For to have a successful relationship both individuals must be single first.

They have to be whole, separate, independent, and fully complete as individuals. For these types of individuals have much to bring to the table. They don't bring baggage to the table, they bring value. Even if baggage arrives, the two of them are equipped to unpack it, organize it, and put things in their proper prospective. **A relationship is only as good as the singles inside it**.

And that is the difference between being unmarried, and being single. So now that you have better understanding… are you single? Or are you simply unmarried?

Chapter 2

Alone But Not Lonely

" And the Lord called unto Adam, Where are you? And Adam said, I heard your voice in the garden, and I was afraid, because I was naked; and I hid myself. And God said, who told you that you were naked?" (genesis 3:9-11)

This scripture is powerful.

Here we see the all-knowing God asking a question. He asked Adam, "where are you?" Now if we are to get the full knowledge of this scripture, we have to understand that God didn't lose Adam. This question was not a matter of location. God asked this question to Adam, with the sole intent to force Adam to do an assessment of where he stood in his circumstance. Adam responded by saying he was naked and afraid, and for those reasons he hid himself. Why is this so powerful? You are about to find out.

Please answer this question. Where are you? Not as far as location. I mean where are you in your singleness? Many of you will say "I am just doing me". Others will say "I never really thought of it." But a mass majority, will quietly utter these words, "I am lonely."

I am lonely. These are words you never thought you'd say. For in the beginning, not being in a relationship was fun. You did what you wanted; whenever you wanted; with who you wanted; and there was no one to answer to. Then, what was fun became the complete opposite. You grew bored of the parties. You were tired of the dating scene. And now having it all out of your system, you've grown fond of the idea of settling down. Maybe not marriage, but just someone to enjoy life with. But when you looked for that *someone*, there was no one. And that's when it hit you, "man, I'm lonely."

Loneliness has haunted men and women to a state of dependency. Many have become so afraid of being lonely, that they hold tight to anyone that will allow them. The thought of being lonely is scary; and no one wants to be its victim.

When you are lonely you have no one to laugh with. You have no one to share your secrets. You cook, and are force to eat by yourself. Loneliness can be cold. Loneliness can be mundane. Loneliness can be depressing.

Loneliness is a place where many unmarried people find themselves after a long period time. Many even conclude being alone, and being lonely as one in the same. This isn't correct. Loneliness is an emotion. And in that truth let me tell you, just because you are unmarried, doesn't mean you are automatically lonely. For there are some married couples that are lonely. In fact, I have counseled lonelier married people, than lonely single people. It has been proven that loneliness can show up no matter the relationship status.

But through revelation from God, and careful research I have discovered that loneliness is not the problem that plagues most people. The real issue is the individual has not mastered being alone. When an individual can master being alone, there is no room for loneliness to come in and cause trauma. But the harsh truth is many people go through loneliness because they don't fully know what it means to be alone.

WHO TOLD YOU THAT?

Loneliness is an emotion that manifests itself due to the thought that says "you are without something"; Or in the case of singleness "someone". In retrospect, loneliness stems from the thought of lack. That then means in order to attack the spirit or emotion of loneliness, we must deal with the root of the issue. The root is the lie that tells you that you are in lack just because you are not in partnership or relationship with another person.

Remember when Adam was asked where he was, he responded "God I am naked so I hid myself." Naked means to be bare or to lack. Do you see how the two conditions are alike? Like many of you, Adam had a problem with loneliness too. When God asked him to assess his life, Adam was really saying "God, I am in lack, and out of fear of being trapped here forever, I hid myself." And when God, heard this, He was angry. He was angry because Adam had been deceived into thinking he was in lack; when in actuality he was made completely whole. But because Adam didn't know this truth, he bought into the lie.

Are you buying into the lie? Have you found yourself hiding in loneliness? Are you so hungry for companionship that you've hidden your morals, values, and dignity just to have someone around? Have you enlisted in the war of loneliness, when you can have the freedom of being alone? Please allow me to pull you out of this bush that you have tucked yourself away in.

Loneliness is not the will of God for you. For to be lonely is to be in lack, and God created you to be whole in every aspect of your life. You are made in the likeness of God, and God lacks nothing. You can't submit to the suggestion of loneliness. Loneliness is a dangerous place. Loneliness is where depression and anxiety breeds. Loneliness forces you to entertain people you shouldn't just to fill the empty spaces. Loneliness will even force you to become someone you are not just to attract the company or attention of others.

Here is the truth: You are unmarried. And you are alone. But that does not mean you are lonely. Who told you that you had to sulk and have a pity party just because you aren't married? Who told you that you needed to have someone around to have a good time? Who told you that a relationship was the key to loneliness?

The truth of the matter is if you are lonely without a partner, you'll be lonely with a partner. The only way to eradicate loneliness from your life is to get rid of the thought that you lack something, and study the beauty of being alone.

Study being Alone

Sounds weird, right? Who studies to be alone? Success singles, that's who. Those that enjoy the benefit of having healthy relationships all understand that there is nothing more powerful than being alone. The reason that not everyone discovers this power is because the term "being alone" has been viewed as a tragedy, when it is the key to freedom.

When we look up Webster's definition of alone, we find that alone means to be separate from others, excluded from others, and solitary. Nowhere do we find terms like "lonely", "hopeless", "pity party" or the like. So, what this emphasizes is alone is not a negative, it merely means to be with yourself. Wow, what a great place to be. Like anyone else, I enjoy going out and spending time with my wife, children, and friends; but I have found that it is nothing like spending time with yourself. In fact, I discovered this truth very early on.

I grew up the only child for nine years, so I know a thing or two about spending time with myself. As an only child for so long, it was imperative that I became rather comfortable with being alone, as I had no other choice. While I would have loved a playmate, a sleeping buddy, and someone to laugh at Barney with, I would not trade the strengths that I gained at such a very young age. I didn't know it then, but my childhood was the genesis for everything that I am today.

Being the only child taught me independence. It geared me to be self-motivated, and helped me to build initiative. My creativity was discovered in my youth. For it took a huge stock of creativity to fill the emptiness of a sibling. I was creating fictional characters, even before I knew what a fairytale or fictional story was. My childhood provided me the opportunity to become fully aware of my potential, my gifts, my weaknesses and strengths, likes and dislikes; it even taught me the language of silence. For in the silence is where being alone tutored me, and helped me to become all one. There were absolutely no distractions in me discovering me.

That is exactly why I encourage everyone to study being alone. Alone is the class that teaches self-understanding. Many people don't like the class of alone. But if they are to ever graduate to the level of friendship, partnership, relationship, and/or marriage, they must pass the class of alone.

Now I'll be the first to point out the obvious, when I say that the class of alone is an extremely difficult course to master. Being alone is challenging, complicated, and chaotic. Only a few of us have mastered the class of alone; and it was a fight every step of the way. The class of alone is one of those classes that will push you to your limits, and force you to truly give your undivided attention. It's not like trigonometry, chemistry, or physics. Sure, these are very difficult courses of study, but they are as elementary as 1+1=2, when compared to the study of alone.

The study of alone is the very detailed, very calculated, and very intricate study of one's self. You have no clue who you are until you commit to being alone. Furthermore, you'll never identify your purposed self until you are willing to be alone.

LANE CHANGE: Alone is not the highlight of absent company, it is the process of becoming all-one.

ALL-ONE : (the place of wholeness)

When you master the class of alone, you will never refer to yourself as "alone" again, but as "all-one." The powerful shift from "alone" to "all-one" is more than a change in pronunciation of the word; but it is a change in the perception of the word. I learned a long time ago that the way you perceive a thing will always determine how you receive that thing. If you presume someone as rude, no matter what they say, or how they phrase their speech and vocabulary, you will still find them rude. Even if they really aren't. This is the gift and curse of perception.

That same principal applies to being alone. For so long "being alone" has been perceived as a negative rather than a positive; because very few individuals possess the vision to see the opportunity inside the opposition. Being so distracted by the opposition of "alone", they never notice the opportunity to become "all-one." There is no way that you can accomplish the goal of being "all-one" without willing to be "alone" for a while.

All-one is the state of wholeness. All-one means you have learned who you are, and you have grown to love and appreciate who you are. All-one means you are familiar with your strengths and weakness. All-one means you know your value, worth, and you aren't willing to compromise them for anyone. All-one means you have located you gifts, and found your purpose. All-one means you don't need the company of another to have fun, feel fulfilled, and/or have validation. A person that is truly all-one doesn't walk around with hopes of finding someone to complete them, because they know they are whole, all by themselves. All-one is the ultimate goal of singleness.

Are you Afraid to be alone?

Not many people ever reach the paradise of being all-one, because they are terrified of being alone. They fear the thought of being lonely, more than they fear the reality of being co-dependent on another. And for this cause do we find countless men and women holding on to relationship that have reached their expiration date a long time ago. There are some that rather hold on to abusers, cheaters, dead beats, and even the spouse of another just to have someone around. But this type of behavior posed a question in my soul that asks, what is it about being alone that terrifies people out of their morals, and dignity? I mean, you rather entertain a fool, than to entertain yourself? Why?

And then, I had what Oprah would describe as an "ah-ha moment." The reason most people are afraid to be alone, is because they are then forced to spend time with the real them.

Are you afraid to be by yourself? Like a child that has watched a horror movie and is now alone in his bedroom, many will, with pounding hearts, reply yes to these questions. But a horror movie to them is no comparison to the horror of who they have become.

When you meet a person, you almost never meet the real them. You meet their representative. You meet the "them" with a mask. You meet the part of them that they want you to see. You meet their accomplishments, their victories, and their best self. But the other part of them is kept secret. You know, the part of them that is flawed. The part that has failed and made mistakes. The part that isn't so lovely. The part that they wish never existed. For while externally you get to see the beauty, internally they are forced to live with the beast. This is why they like having the company of others, because this is the only time they have relief from the person they really are. Being with you provides them safety, for when they are alone, they are left with a monster.

Chapter 3

The Beasts of Being Alone

I am a firm believer that in all of your getting, get an understanding. The knowledge of a thing is never enough; the power is in the understanding. I mean, I can give you countless pieces of wisdom on how to maximize being all-one; but if I don't explain how to apply them, you'll still be left in the same predicament. Understanding leads to better cooperation. The understanding of a thing teaches you what to expect; this way if and when the negative arrives you aren't surprised. When you understand the pros and cons you are better equipped to embrace them. Being all-one must be understood.

With this being said, I need you to understand that when you make the choice to be all-one (emphasizes on choice) many beast will come out of the wilderness. Remember, being alone can be scary, confusing, and troublesome and these beasts that I am about to mention are the leading cause of why most people never reach the place of becoming all-one. Now when they run, they aren't intending to run from their self-discovery; but inevitably do so when they avoid being alone.

INSECURITY:

An extremely dangerous beast that will growl and seek to devour you before you can become all one is insecurity. When a person is alone for a lengthy period of time, or beyond the time they intended, insecurities began to stir up in their mind. They begin to consider "maybe it's me"; "Maybe I have the problem"; "maybe I'm not the girlfriend type"; "maybe husband is a title I will never wear". Then, the questions begin to surface asking, "What did I do?" "What could I have done to keep him/her around?" "What did I say?" "Where did things go wrong?"

Friend, one of the most dangerous things you could do to yourself, while you are alone, is to begin blaming yourself for the departure of others. If a person walks out of your life, they simply weren't called to stay. For I have discovered in my own life that when someone is really meant to stay they won't be able to leave. And when you identify that a person is not meant to stay, the best thing to do is let them go.

LANE CHANGE: Some people in our life have an expiration date. And you should never hold on to someone after their expiration date has passed, because that's when things get stinky.

Also, when people are truly called to be in your life they are planted. Just like a tree planted in the ground, they are there no matter the weather. This means, come hail, snow, thunderstorm, or tornado, they remain planted. So, if a person is able to walk out of your life, the conclusion should never be "it's all my fault they're gone"; but the verdict inside you must rather conclude "not planted."

Going forward, people that are planted don't have a problem staying rooted. If you are surrounded by individuals that are on the see-saw of "in one day, and out the next", they aren't planted either. These individuals are just fond of the idea of being planted. But the idea of being planted and the actuality of being planted are so very different. Again, **this is not a question of you, but it is a revelation of them.**

When a person is planted they are willing to take you with your assets and your liabilities. No, they don't just hang around because of what you can offer, or because of what you can do for them. For this is a clear sign that they aren't in love with the tree (in this instance the tree is you) but they are in love with the fruit the tree bears. And when you (the tree) stop bearing fruit, they're gone. Reflecting that they never wanted the tree, but the fruit. *Are you entertaining people that are only around to eat your fruit?*

A person that is planted, appreciates all that you have to offer, but they don't become a leech. This is because they are more interested in being a tree that bears good fruit for you. This is powerful, because while you are yet alone, you should still consider the type of trees that you'll have in your forest. And having trees that bear fruit for you, simply means that you have people around that help you become greater.

If you have a person in your life right now that has been encouraging you to be single, or who may have even given you this book on singleness, that person is a tree bearing good fruit for you. They aren't hoping you don't ever find someone, they just have the courage to tell you "not now." A tree bearing good fruit for you has your best interest at heart, and only want the absolute best for you. This means when they tell you something that is uncomfortable for you to receive, remember it was equally, if not more, uncomfortable for them to tell you. And while this person doesn't always agree with every person you date or everything that you do; understand that they aren't being a hater, they are being honest. These types of people are highly necessary in your life.

Now let's look at the flip side. As important as it is to have people that appreciate your assets, it is equally as important to surround yourself with people that are strong enough to take on your liabilities. Often times, we blame liabilities as the reason people divorce friendships and relationships. But this all goes back to being plant. Like a tree that can handle the worst storm, planted people can endure your worst storm. When a storm comes you don't see a tree uprooting itself and running for cover. On the contrary, you see that tree standing! No matter how cold, how wet, or how treacherous the winds blow, it stands. On the hottest day of summer, with the sun beaming right over it, that tree stands. Friend, you MUST surround yourself with people that are built to stand!

These people aren't scared of your limitations. They aren't bothered by your weaknesses. Neither do they lose their loyalty, at the same time you lose your temper. Planted people can take the heat! And they don't spend time criticizing you, or judging you for your mistakes and flaws. Planted people can handle your cracks, and broken pieces; because they realize they have some leaks themselves. Boy, do you need these types of people in your life. These essential people, like nurses, spend time helping you stabilize, instead of leaving you to drown in your insecurities. You sharpen them, and they sharpen you in exchange. These individuals are vital on your quest to be all one. Now if you have not located this types of planted people, I encourage you to stay alone until you do.

Jealousy:

Another beast that creeps out in the wilderness, while you are alone is the beast of jealousy. Now when I tell people that I mentor on singleness to watch out for jealousy, they often scoff at the idea of them ever being jealous. They can't picture themselves being jealous of another person and their happiness. And my response is, "give it time." It is something about wanting something for so long and you never get it. It's something about trying to get yourself together, and you still get looked over. You bought the dress. Put on the suit. Wore the cologne. Curled your hair. And yet you still go home alone. If given enough time, the thing you scoffed at earlier, could very well be the thing you struggle with later. And the happiness of others, if you aren't careful, could become your torment.

Not because you are hateful. Not because you're evil. It is because the thing, you want so badly, appears to not want you in return. And whenever you see someone enjoying the very thing you desperately wish to have, it births envy, even without your consent. Yes, jealousy will come in without your permission. And sometimes it comes in without you noticing.

Another wedding where you play the role of a bridesmaid. Sure, you support your friend and you smile; oh but, behind that smile, you wonder when your special day will arrive, and you get the chance to marry your prince. After a couple of your girlfriends' weddings as a bridesmaid, you'll still have that beautiful smile on your face, beaming with joy, but the shine that will be even brighter is the subtle gleam of jealousy in your eyes. You'll put on mascara, and even some eye shadow; but the shimmer of green will still appear, even when it's not the wedding colors.

Or you, the good guy, with everything going on, and everything together; it gets cold in the house alone doesn't it? No matter how nice the layout of the house is, and no matter what décor you have, you notice it's still not a home. Only a woman can make a house a home. How do you know this? Because all of your fellas, have found their women. And while you're still reminiscing about the late nights, and laughs, and watching the game; they are at home, cuddling up on the sofa watching a movie with their ladies, planning their future. All while you sit in wonder of if your future will be spent solo. Then, as you think you're alone in the house, if you look hard enough you'll begin to notice jealousy creeping threw your backdoor, coming to keep you company.

While I don't wish jealousy to come upon you, I have to warn you that it will, if you neglect to keep your eyes on the big picture. The big picture while you are alone is to become all one. This means studying yourself, learning yourself, and evolving into the best expression of yourself. Being whole without the need of another. So, you have to be clear that right now, you don't need the company of another. You are to use this time to become familiar and comfortable with yourself. And when you completely accept that this alone time is necessary, you will begin to find yourself so indulged in the discovery of yourself, that you don't even have time for another. So, this minimizes the desire for company; and you won't be tempted to be jealous when you see others and their partners. You will look and smile genuinely. But this time it won't be with an eye of jealousy; rather it will be with an eye of fulfilment because you have the wonderful company of yourself.

Bitterness:

Bitterness is a beast that is very similar to the beast of jealousy. It has some of the same traits and characteristics, but the thing about bitterness is it makes you mean. Bitterness is more vocal and more obvious than jealousy. You become unpleasant when you're bitter. Because you don't have company of your own, you will find yourself speaking down about those that do. You'll become that man/woman that hates valentine's day, sweetest day, love stories, and/or love songs. You will become as the scrooge of love; yelling bah humbug to anyone that has a significant other. When you become bitter about being alone, you become the spokesperson of how all men are dogs and how all women are gold diggers. But in actuality, none of that is true. You're just bitter because you're alone.

One of the worst things you can do while you are studying to be all-one, is to use this time where you are supposed to become better, to become bitter. Bitterness is not a good trait to pick up. Because your alone time is only for a set time; but if you become bitter, it lingers on even after your alone time is complete. And then when you enter to the place where you are ready to have another in your life, you still won't;

because you have become so bitter to the point that no one wants to be around you.

Bitterness creates a place for abandonment. Yes, people will leave you. No one wants to be around a bitter person. Bitterness will even run away your family and friends. You will look around and see that people are literally avoiding you, because being around you is so draining and depressing. Bitterness will make you the worst expression of yourself; and it will block you from ever enjoying the life you were purposed to live. Please do yourself a favor, don't get bitter.

How? How can you not get bitter? I am so glad you asked. You can only be tempted to do the thing that you consider. If you consider good, you will do good. If you consider bad, you will do bad. The scripture reminds us that "as we think so are we." We become the thing we think about. So, the protection from growing bitter is to not consider it. You must use this alone time to only consider the good that will come from it, which we will discuss in a moment. Think of how much better you will be. Don't think anything negative about the process of becoming all-one. When bitter thoughts begin to arise, simple ignore them, and **say out of your mouth**, "*it is well, and I will be better after this.*"

LANE CHANGE: Your confession to become better, will defeat the suggestion to become bitter.

Complication:

There's a beast that has harassed us since we were babies. From learning to breastfeed. To learning to crawl. To learning to walk. To school years, taking test. To teenage years, dealing with hormones and peer pressure. To adulthood, learning to budget, pay bills, and trying not to sink in it all. This beast has been there every step of the way; and his name is complication.

On this journey of being all one, single, and the best expression of yourself, you will find that the discoveries will be endless. You will learn things about yourself that you never even knew. You will discover gifts that you had no idea that you had. You are on a journey to reveal all the hidden mysteries that God placed on the inside of you when he created you. Through this journey, you will discover how whole you can become, all without the company of another.

Now while all this sounds nice, fine, and lovely, I want you to know that the journey from being "alone" to being "all one"" is very complex. The reason being is because we as humans are very complex. To try to figure things out would take much time and much focus. And this is why you have to take this journey alone; if you tried to take another, with their opinions and views, it would make a complex task, all the more confusing.

If you are going to take on this highly beneficial task of becoming all-one you have to be willing to deal with complications. I have found that **where there is ignorance, complication is born**. Now I am not in any way degrading you or attacking your intelligence. But seeing as though we did not create ourselves, and with the overwhelming number of people that don't know their purpose in life; we are very ignorant about our make-up. While we know quite a bit about ourselves, none of us can conclude that we have the answer to everything in our life. With this partial ignorance, much like partial vision, we run head on into complications.

Complications are stumbling blocks, problems, obstacles, and confusions. Complications come in the form of questions like "why didn't my marriage work?" "Will I ever have a baby?" "Why do I get so angry?" "Why can't I trust people?" "Why am I so guarded?" "What is my purpose?" "What can I offer the world?" And when we try to answer these types of questions, the term complicated is an understatement. This is why it is vital to spend this alone time, with God, our creator, so that he can give insight to the who's, what's, when's, and why's about your life. This is the only way that we stand a chance against the beast of complication. The scripture says "if anyone lacks wisdom, let him ask of the Lord." He is the only one with the answers to the very complicated questions about your life. Maximize being alone, and talk to God.

Dependency:

The beast that is my 2nd most hated of all is the beast of dependency. I would say about 85% of the unmarried people that I counsel struggle with the beast of dependency. Dependency is the direct opposite of what being all-one is. People that are dependent are addicts. And while their addiction is not tied to alcohol, or drugs; they have found themselves hooked on another substance. They are hooked on the acceptance, approval, validation, and initiation of other people.

Individuals that are dependent on others have a very difficult time to become all-one, because they have conditioned themselves to wait on the green light from others before they make any moves. Dependent people aren't hard to spot out. If you aren't a dependent person, I am sure you know a dependent person. These are people that believe that they need the company of others before they can have a good time. Before they can laugh. Before they can go to dinner. Before they can try a new task. They hate being at home alone. They have to either have someone with them, or be on the phone with someone. Their entire life is at the beck and call of other people.

There is a reason that we were all born alone. God didn't intend for us to be dependent upon anyone. I am not saying you have to deny the help of others; but I am saying our well-being, and the flow of our life should not be governed by anyone but ourselves. No one should have control over our happiness, potential, progress, or destiny, but we ourselves. Whenever we take on a partner, friend, or spouse, whatever they bring to the table should be an addition to what we already have, and not an initiation of what we believe we were missing.

LANE CHANGE: When you are dependent on another you are not all-one,

*you are **ALL THEM**.*

Settlement & Compromise:

While dependency is my 2nd most hated beast; Settlement & Compromise has the race summed up for 1st place. If you make the choice to never study to be all-one, there is no way you can access singleness. As a result, you will be bound to be devoured by settlement and compromise. Settlement and compromise is destined to the individual who fails to realize their fullest potential, power, and purpose.

When you don't know who you are, a person can shrink you into anything they want. When you don't know how strong you are, you will live life defeated and weak. When you have no clue of your purpose, you will be employed to help someone else fulfill theirs. When you don't unveil your value and worth, you will accept the crumbs on the floor, when you were called to eat at the table.

These are the people working jobs that are beneath them; making money that doesn't even equate a percentage their value. These are the women that settle for abusive, insecure, poor excuses for men. And instead of leaving the joker, they settle and have babies with him; and as a result they teach their children to playout this same settlement when they are older. These are the men that play video games all day, sleep majority of the day, and their only source of income is the drugs they sell on the corner. Not knowing that they are settling. They have no knowledge that if they can successfully sell drugs, they can harbor those same skill sets and oversee a business. Oh, but their excuses shoot down that idea.

Settlement and compromise devours the dreams, chews on the vision, and digests the future of the one that refuses to go after more. We have to stop settling in all areas. I know this is a singleness book. But allow me the opportunity to get this off my chest. We have to stop settling as men, women, parents, children, friends, dreamers, leaders, and whatever other roles we carry out. Settlement and compromise are the tools we use to build regret, frustration, and contention.

You were created by God to be complete and whole. You were created to be all-one and single. You were created to live an abundant life. You were created on purpose, with a purpose. You are not a mistake, failure, or reject. You are a child of the King; and it is time you stop settling and start soaring! Drake said it best when he said, "you only live once". The world went crazy off the song, but very few took the lyrics to heart, and searched after their destiny. Allow me to repeat it for you, **<u>YOU ONLY LIVE ONCE!</u>** Stop settling and compromising, and go capture all the beauties of your life.

Chapter 4

The Beauties of Being Alone

While there are many beasts that accompany being alone; there are many great beauties of being alone. In fact, I believe that when we are alone, if we begin to magnify the beauties of being alone, we minimize and overshadow all the potential beasts of being alone. Again, the success of going from being "alone" to becoming "all-one" will rely heavily on our perception during the process. You have to see the treasures inside your alone time, or else you enter into friendships, partnerships, and/or relationships prematurely to you becoming all one; and the union is ruined even before it begins. Only those that are willing to be alone for a little while can handle the responsibility and privilege of connecting with another.

Me-search:

This beauty is the heartbeat for this book and this chapter, and it is an absolute necessity for becoming all one. Being alone, provides you with the chance to get to know yourself. Without distractions. From our birth into the world, we have spent countless amounts of time, energy, and brain activity trying to figure out other people. This was not something that we were taught, this was something that came natural. We were born into the world, with a built-in ability to study the people and the things around us. From infant months, up until toddler age, all of our learning was pure observation and study. We didn't talk, all we did was observe, while making mental notes. This authentic study was powerful.

We first began to study our parents. When learned who mom was. Who dad was. We learned their different personalities and behaviors. And this all came from just being held, fed, and changed. We learned so much just by being in their presence. Then, we took on the task of learning our siblings. We learned them, and their diverse characteristics, like with our parents, by spending time. After playtime, lunch time, nap time, bath time, and bedtime we pretty much knew our sibling(s) inside and out. And in between the sibling rivalry, we learned that our sibling(s) were our first best friend(s).

After earning a bachelor's from studying the people inside our home. We went on to earn a master's in studying the people outside our home. We studied grandparents, aunts, uncles, cousins, god-parents, and other extended family members. Then, as time went on we studied teachers, friends, enemies, boy/girlfriends, etc. So many different people crossed our path that never even knew they were the subject of discovery. But with no mention at all, we studied them. We made conclusions, formed ideas, built prejudices, and this was all done mainly by pure observation and study.

Now I applaud the study of others. I think it is very important to know the people that you are surrounded by, and spend time with. For this could be very critical to your advancement into your purpose, and you truly living the life you were created to live. But one thing that I think is ten times more important, and is even more critical to your purposed being carried out, is the study of yourself. While we devote so much into the study of other people, it distracts us from the research of "me". This study is what I like to call "me-search."

Being alone, offers a chance for us to dig deep into who we are, find our true self, and live a more full and purposed life. Not knowing who you are is very dangerous; because when you don't fully understand who you are, anyone can come along and craft you into whatever they desire you to be. And my friend, you are too unique and God has too much planned for you, for you to just become a minimal version of another person's ideas and expectations.

Being alone, gives you a chance to learn your value, your gifts, and your contributions. This is key because you cannot perform at your highest level, without knowing your strengths and God given greatness. I have found that a person is only great to the level of discovery. If you only conclude you have a level one greatness, you perform at that level. Just as so, a person does at a level ten. Your ability to do great things, and have great successes, is all a result of the "me-search" that you are willing to put in. I'll give you an example: one of my biggest role models is Steve Harvey. Mr. Harvey started his career as a comedian. And he spoke about how he just wanted to be a great comedian. Now being one of the Original Kings of Comedy, I'd say he accomplished that. But the thing I love about Steve Harvey is he didn't settle on one level of greatness. While he was a great comedian, he heard an inner call for more. And studying his life, Mr. Harvey has taught me to never be afraid to reinvent yourself. And with answering the call for more, we witnessed him go from one level of greatness to the next. He went from comedian, to a radio host, to an actor, to a fashion designer, to an author, to a game show host, to a daytime television personality, and those are just the things we get to witness publicly. He did, what I had to learn, and what I am encouraging you to do. He did some "me-search". He took the time to learn all the things that made him great. He discovered his gifts and his purpose. And while doing so, he entered into new levels of greatness, and now he is living a life that is admired by millions.

What great person are you missing the opportunity to meet? How long will you avoid the meeting with your best self? You have yet to discover the person you could be. You have yet to discover your greatness. You have yet to unlock the door to the person that will lead you to your destiny. There is a better you, inside of you. There is a dreamer inside you. There is a visionary inside you. There is an innovator inside you. There is a more loving person inside you. There is a more generous person inside you. And there is someone waiting for the "now you" to meet the "best you." There is someone waiting for you to realize your greatness. For when you become the best that you can be, your life becomes a testament, that others can also.

Your "me-search" is necessary. Not just for you, but for the people you will inspire. You've done the work of studying others; now you have to learn yourself. You have to study to find out your strengths and weaknesses. Knowing your strengths teaches you where you excel. Being aware of your weaknesses remind you of the areas that need improvement. You also, have to go into "me-search" to unveil your area of gifting. What do you do well? Do you sing? Write? Decorate? What is it that makes you phenomenal? You have to find these answers.

Many people live and die with their gifts unopened. And because of this there are best-selling books never written. Classic songs never sung. Block buster movies never produced. Fortune 500 businesses never started. When they were buried their purpose was buried also. They never utilized their gift, and never reached their destiny. **This can't be your story!** You have too much inside of you to keep it there. I encourage you to go on a hunt. Hunt to find what God has giving you to share with the world. Hunt to find what makes you special. Hunt to find the thing you love to do, that you'll do for free. Hunt to find the thing that will bring your life fulfillment and esteem. Hunt to find the things that make you a cut above the rest.

LANE CHANGE: Me-search is the course that every great person took; and the course that every defeated person refused to take.

Identified Purpose:

When you take on the opportunity to be alone, the beauty of discovering your purpose is identified. Yes, your purpose. That thing you were born to do. Purpose is a topic that people have struggled with for ages. Everyone wants to know the anchoring question of "why am I here?" And until that question locates the answer, we live life aimlessly and without cause. Being alone affords you the opportunity to discover the "why" about your life.

I always recommend being alone to find your purpose, because it cuts out distractions. Too often we allow people to speak their opinions into our lives, and we grab our purpose from them. Or we look around at what we do for a living, and we conclude our purpose from that. Or we look around at what we do well, and we use that as the parallel of our purpose. But this is not wise. Just because we make a living doing something, or because we do a thing well, that doesn't mean it is our purpose. Your living is, in most cases, the thing you are paid for; while your purpose is the thing that you're made for. And the thing you do well, could just be a gift that helps you to reach your purpose, not become your purpose itself.

The opinion of others, and the conclusions that they have drawn on your purpose is null and void also. Now we are creations, created by the creator. And it has always puzzled me why one creation, would turn to another creation to get insight on their purpose. How would they know this? They, like you, are a creation. They are having a tough enough time trying to discover their own purpose, so what makes them a scholar on your purpose? If you are to ever figure out why you were created and what you are purposed to do, you must consult with the one who created you and gave you your purpose. For only he knows why he created you. Why he created you at this time. Why he gave you your type of upbringing. Why he put you in that family. Why you struggle in certain areas. Why you do what you do so well. Why you act how you act. He created you. He gave you your purpose. And he wants to reveal that purpose to you.

My friend, you are not a mistake. You are not an error. You are not just here to roam the earth purposelessly and die. No, you were created on purpose to carry out a purpose. This is why you weren't aborted, miscarried or still born. This is why you didn't die in the crib. This is why the accident couldn't take your life. This is why you woke up today. This is why you grabbed this book. It is all because of you are purposed. Your continuation of life, is proof that God still has something that he needs you to do. God grants us a new day, with the sole intent for us to continue in our purpose. For our purpose is the very reason for the life he gave us. And for that same cause we remain living.

Purpose is the thin line between living a fulfilled life, and a mundane life. When you know your purpose, and are living in it, life is amazing. Life is exciting, happy, and rich. There is no bad day for a person living their purpose; for even a bad day is a good day, because they know that it works for their good in the end. But woe to the person who never learns their purpose. They are forced to live a life of boredom, frustration, and turmoil. Oh, how horrific it is to sense that there is more available, but never manifesting it. Purpose is the key to real living. For I am a firm believer that until you enter into your purpose, you are not living, you are merely existing. And Jesus came that we may have life, not existence.

LANE CHANGE: Spend this time alone, to speak with God, and allow him to expose his purpose for your creation.

Once God exposes his purpose for your life, you are now granted a standard. And once you receive your purpose, you now have a qualifier that instructs you on what/who should and shouldn't be in your life. Your purpose gives you direction, value, and worth. And those standards weed out all the things that don't make the cut. When you know your purpose there are certain things you are no longer willing to do. For example, if you learn your purpose is to be a singer, you won't jeopardize that purpose with drinking and smoking. Your purpose has raised the standard. Likewise, when you know that you are purposed to live as an eagle, you won't spend time flocking with chickens. Your purpose will highlight areas of mediocrity. And because of the tugging of purpose, you will find it very difficult to settle or hold on to something/someone that doesn't fit your purpose.

    I know this all too well. Before I devoted my life to living my purpose, I was stuck doing everything else. I was befriending people that I knew weren't tied to my purpose. I dated people I knew that couldn't compliment my purpose. I carried habits that I knew weren't connected to my purpose. I was entertaining purposeless conversation, television, and activities. God exposed me to my purpose when I was 18years old in college. I was home for summer and while working a summer job, God spoke to me about my purpose of helping people get beyond their current setback or negative circumstance. At this time, he showed me how my purpose would partially be expressed through my gift to write. Now, while I've always known I had a gift to write, even at the age of 7, I never knew that it would tie into my purpose. That summer God had informed me how my ability to write would better equip me to live my purpose.

Now, even with this new knowledge of my purpose, I didn't jump right into it. I continued to do what I called normal; but in actuality it was abnormal. And being honest, it was horrible. Why? Because instead of me running with what God had shared, I ran from it in fear. I thought "wait, I can't be a writer. I can't inspire people to get beyond where they are. God, you must have the wrong person." So, I ran. I ran to other jobs, and I tried to hide away in school. Now while I was a dean's list student in college, financially things got extremely difficult; forcing me to have to leave school. This was hard for me; but God came to me and shared, "your purpose is not connected to that path." Then, I said "ok, I will find a good job." And I did. In fact, I found several. But the thing was, I'd get a good job, love it at first, and then not long after, I found myself dreading it and even hating the job I once loved. After quitting jobs, and after being laid off from a few, God spoke to me and said "your purpose is not connected to that path. Your purpose is directly connected to me."

So right away the light came on. Now I knew why I grew to hate the jobs that I once loved. While they offered good money, they provided nothing for my purpose. While the people I worked with were nice, they didn't fit anywhere in my purpose. Now, you'd think that with this added knowledge I would go ahead and devote myself to my purpose. But oh, not me. At this time of revelation, I was married with children, and I had my attention glued to my responsibilities as a husband and father. So, I had to work. With this in mind I went after more jobs, only to get the same outcome. Then, God came to me and blew my mind. He very clearly spoke to me the thing I need you to know "I pay for what I order."

This was the moment that changed my life forever. God told me "he pays for what he orders." What this means is if he called you to do a thing, he will provide everything you need to successfully carry it out. And my faith in God, had grown to a point where it ran away all of my fears. And when I made the choice to live my purpose, all sorts of doors flung open, and while I still felt some fear, God never ceased to provide for me and my family. He ordered me to live this purpose, and when I cooperated, he provided my every need.

Now why did I tell you this? Because right now you are operating in things that are in no way tied to your purpose.

There are people in your life that you know are not tied to your purpose. There are habits that you have that threaten your purpose. There are companies, jobs, churches, groups, and other teams that you are connected to that aren't related to your purpose. Even without you fully knowing your purpose, you know this. How? Because no matter how good things are at times, something on the inside of you says, "it's not good enough."

LANE CHANGE:

There is an inward cry for more. There is an instinct to increase, and an intuition that something is missing. And that thing is called "purpose."

The reason why you aren't thrilled. The reason why you are quickly and easily bored with these things/people. The reason you feel unfulfilled or complacent. And the reason you feel like there is more to life; is because there absolutely is. God has more to give you than what you have right now. And it will all be made accessible to you the moment you enter into your purpose. So, how long will you run from discovering your purpose? Do yourself a favor, spend this alone time, discovering your purpose. I promise your life will never be the same.

Venting Opportunity:

One of the greatest beauties that you will discover and grow to appreciate with being alone, is the beauty of being able to vent without being judged. Venting in private gives you the opportunity to get things off your chest; and allows you the chance to display emotional outburst without repercussion of others. When you are alone you get the opportunity to yell, cry, throw things, complain, and act a complete nut, and then recollect yourself without anyone ever knowing. Being the only child I learned this treasure very early. When I was a child I was tough. I never cried, never complained, and rarely showed any emotion at all. Well, one day I was in my grandmother's kitchen, and a cousin of mine, thought it would be funny to sneak up on me and scare me. And when he did I jump so hard, that it knocked down a full can of paint down on my 8-year-old foot. At the time, I had never felt such a pain. While I was able to compose my emotions in front of him; I remember running down to the basement, alone, and bawling my eyes out.

I was a lion in the face of my cousin, but I was a lamb in private. However, this painful moment provided me the exposure of venting. I needed that alone time. I needed to be alone to cry. I needed to be alone in my weak moment. Had someone seen me in my weakness, they may have mistaken my weak moment, as a part of my character. Isn't it funny how people can see you in a weak moment, and immediately place labels on you? Just because they meet you unemployed, they label you lazy. Just because they catch you in a financial bind, they label you poor or broke. I have learned that you can never judge a person when they are in transition. For they have not manifested into their true self yet, they are simply in transition to becoming it.

While you are on your journey to being single and all-one, remember you are still in transition. And in your transition, you will say and do things out of emotionalism. You will be frustrated at times. Moody at times. Sad at times. Confused at times. Angry at times. And when you are going through these changes, it is best to do it alone. Being alone provides you the freedom to vent, without being forced to relive it later. Venting is a very powerful process. Venting allows you the chance to blow off steam, and refocus. Venting is the act of relinquishing your weaknesses, mistakes, flaws, and failures; and then starting fresh from that point forward.

This reminds me of my childhood. I am sure you can all relate to being chastised by a parent, and then going to your room. Now while in front of your parent, you were silent as a church mouse, but in you room, all alone, you had tons to say. Now you never said it where they could hear you, but you let it all out when you were alone. Funny, now that we think about it; but we have to admit, this alone time, gave us the chance to say what we wanted, and stay out of trouble all at the same time.

Again, venting is a process that is best left for closed doors. There is nothing worse than venting publicly. When you vent publicly, you may get it all out, and you may be done, but the people that witnessed your vent will always carry the memory. And now you find yourself forced to prove that the way you carried on was not you, but you were simply having a bad moment.

Everyone needs the privacy to be alone with their weaknesses. Not to hide them, but to deal with them without interference. The acknowledgement of these weaknesses is already hard enough, but when you add the judgment and speculation of others, it upgrades from a fight to an all-out war. Not to mention the commentary and opinions that others will give about your situation. Because regardless to whether you are "just venting" and needing and ear to listen, that ear comes accompanied by a mouth. It is very rare that one will listen without forming an opinion or stating their thoughts. The reason being is they think since you involved them, it gives them the green light to go and give you their take. And this only leaves you confused, misguided, or worse, handling things the way they would instead of the way you see fit yourself. It is never wise to handle matters about your life the way another would. They don't live your life and can only give you generic tools to fix a problem that requires tools from the manufacturer.

What does this mean? Well consider this, you are driving a Rolls Royce. It's beautiful but one day while you're driving you notice that there is a loud ticking under the hood every time you reach a certain speed. Then, you think "hey I need to figure this out". Now a Rolls Royce is not a common car. It is a very expensive luxury car and it is tailor fit for the driver. You love your vehicle, and you want it running and performing at its absolute best. You aren't handy enough to fix the issue. So, what do you do?

Do you try to fix your vehicle yourself, even though you know you are clueless of the issue? Do you take your vehicle to a friend to work on? Do you take your vehicle to a family mechanic to do some diagnostics? I am sure you answered "no" to each of these questions. There is no way that you would take your very expensive car that you love and try to fix it yourself. And the chances of your taking it to someone else to fix on is even more ridiculous. Now, what do you do? You take it back to the manufacturer. They made the Rolls Royce so they are more than capable of handling any issues that occur with the Rolls Royce. Any tools or equipment they need they don't have to search outside the warehouse because they have everything necessary to correct the dilemma and get you back running.

Is not your life of greater value than a Rolls Royce? So why then do we try to repair our issues ourselves? Why do we take our life to others to work on and diagnose? Why do we look to family members to provide answers to questions that only our manufacturer knows?

Friends, we must treat our life as the priceless commodity that it is. You are rare. You are not common. You are wonderful and irreplaceable. You are an original and if you are to fix the issues in your life and get back running and performing as your best self you have to go back to the manufacturer. Jesus is our manufacturer. He knows how you are. He knows what tools he needs when you are broken. He knows what words you need to hear when you're discouraged. He is skilled at putting your life together when things fall apart. He made you and he knows you. And if you are to ever become all that you have the potential to be you have to neglect from venting to others and vent to him. But instead of being misguide and confused, he is the one that will provide knowledge, understanding and wisdom. Knowledge on what the issue is. Understanding on why you have the issue. And wisdom on how to resolve it.

Venting is a powerful tool that helps you get it all out; however, venting is made of most effect when released into capable hands and his name is Jesus.

Take this alone time to vent. This is an opportunity for you to say ugly things, do ugly things and no one be hurt by them. This is an opportunity for you to be Clark Kent, instead of struggling to remain Superman. Your venting opportunities, when you are alone, provides you the release therapy everyone needs.

Permission to Be You:

Another beauty of being alone is you get the opportunity to grant yourself permission to be you. I know that sounds crazy, but not everyone has given themselves the permission to be them. Some people are afraid to be them. They fear what others may think, say, or conclude about them. Many are afraid to highlight their weakness and struggles. They feel that they have to live this "armor" type lifestyle that declares nothing bothers them, or that they don't have room for improvement.

Reversely, others are afraid to show their strengths and potential. They are afraid to be great. They are nervous about soaring and reaching their highest heights. Why? Because they don't really know if they have what it takes to obtain or maintain a life of success. Another reason that relates to this type of fear is some people are afraid that others will find them to be uppity or high-class. They fear the speech from people that says "you've changed", "you must think you're better than us", and/or the question "who do you think you are?"

Because of these fears, many live prohibited and imprisoned. Their body has become their prison. And their greater self has been locked away, because they have failed to give themselves the permission to be them. Have you given yourself permission to be you? Or have you denied yourself, and crafted a life to please others?

LANE CHANGE: *Give yourself permission to be YOU.*

You have to give yourself permission to live your purpose. Give yourself permission to be ok with not knowing everything. Give yourself permission to make mistakes. Give yourself permission to win. Give yourself permission to have, be and do more. Give yourself permission to be unique. Give yourself permission to not fit in. Give yourself permission to live a life without the need for approval, validation, and acceptance. Give yourself permission to become all one. Give yourself permission to live single.

Once you give yourself permission to be you, you grant yourself the freedom to live a fulfilled and happy life. People that are miserable, and dreadful are that way because they have not given themselves permission to live a joyful life. They rather wait for someone else to come along and provide that luxury for them. This cannot be your story! Never wait for someone to come along to give you permission to be you. For you could be waiting a lifetime. Don't submit yourself to a life sentence of unhappiness. Don't compromise your freedom to be you, just to satisfy another. Be you! And if anyone can't accept you for being you, so be it!

The worse thing in the world is to be a people pleaser. Because even with your devotion to please everybody, there will always be somebody that still has an issue. They don't like your hairstyle, your outfit, your career choice. There will always be someone that will look for a reason to discredit you. When you deny yourself, for the sake of others, you not only limit yourself, but you enlist yourself into a life of being someone that you are not. And my friend, let me tell you it is so much easier to be yourself, than it is to carry on in a lie.

God made you to be exactly the way you are. He didn't make a mistake. You aren't useless. You were supposed to have your personality; your humor; your style; your thought process; your attitude; your gifts; your sensitivity; your boldness. Who you are is exactly who you need to be to live and carry out your purpose. When God made you, he made you just the way you needed to be to complete your destiny. And your destiny is dependent on you being you, and not anyone else. God wants you to be a marvelous original, and not a second-rate version of someone else. When you conform to being what others want you to be, you live out their purpose; while yours is left to die. And all the while you are frustrated, angry, and suffocating on the inside.

Lastly, many find it hard to be them, because they don't want to disappoint. They devote themselves to living in such a way that it lines up with who their parents want them to be, or who they believe others expected them to be. And once they have a mind set on allowing others to live vicariously through them, they often fail at being who they truly desire to be. Now while it is good to make others proud, it is never ok to do so at the expense of you denying yourself the opportunity to become your best self.

This is the goal, when becoming all-one and single. To become the person you were destined to be; and to love that person. The reason many fail at reaching their purpose, and at loving the skin they are in, is because they are distracted with being who others say they are. So, they wear clothes that they really don't like. Form habits they know they shouldn't, but for the sake of being cool, they do so anyway. They perform for applauds from others by marketing their body parts, misbehaving, and following the latest trends. But all the while they grow to become people they hate, and wish they hadn't. Again, don't fall victim to this disease. Do yourself a favor, permit yourself to be you! I promise, you are going to love the person you become. And others will appreciate you also.

Awakening of Greatness:

One final beauty that I believe you owe it to yourself to master before you enter into a friendship, partnership, or relationship is the beauty of being great solo. I value very highly the power of togetherness with other people. I think that when two or more people get in agreement and work together, combining their gifts and skills, that great things can truly be manifested. This makes me consider groups like New Edition, The Beatles, Destiny's Child, and TLC. These groups were amazing, and they worked together to create great music. Then, I begin to consider teams like the Chicago Bulls, LA Lakers, and Miami Heat. The players of these teams, for years, have worked together to win games, and earn many championship titles. Lastly, I consider companies like Apple, Coca-Cola, and General Mills. All of these companies consist of individuals that creatively work together to create products that we have all grown to love and appreciate.

    While I admired the togetherness of all these groups, teams, and companies, I couldn't help but wonder how they were able to become so successful. I mean, with all the different personalities, attitudes, egos, and ideas, how did they make it work? How do you form a dynamic singing group like the Beatles? How do you mold a dream team as great as the Chicago Bulls? How do you build a brand as big as Apple? Then, the light went off. Before there was a "we", there was a "me." Inside the Beatles there was a Paul McCartney. Inside the Chicago Bulls there was a Michael Jordan. And inside the mega company, "Apple", there was Steve Jobs.

It wasn't the great marketing plans for "Apple" that manifested their greatness. It wasn't the coaching technics of the "Bulls" that manifested their greatness. And it wasn't the song selection of "the Beatles" that manifested their greatness. No, *the secret ingredient to building a great team, is the gathering of great individuals.* The power of any team, group, friendship, or relationship is always found inside the individuals.

This is where you are now. You are in the stage of becoming a great individual. Understand that no one can initiate your greatness, they can only be an addition to your greatness. Same is true about you for someone else. The key in this stage of your life is to identify your greatness. This requires honesty and dedication. I say this because in discovering all the great things about yourself, you also discovery all the not so great things about yourself.

Take this time to do a complete inspection of you. Are you creative? Are you hard working? Are you reliable? Are you flexible? What are your skills?? Talents? Gifts? You have to find out all the things that make you valuable. I don't care what others may have spoken into your life that has made you question your value; you are great! And when you begin to unveil all of your qualities of greatness, you will be powerful.

Knowing your greatness increases your confidence. Builds your esteem. And pushes you into a leader mindset. The awareness of your greatness helps you to boldly stand alone, without the need of another. Great individuals aren't dependent on someone acknowledging them. They just walk in their greatness and the acknowledgement of others follows.

Paul McCartney was great way before the Beatles were formed. Before he was a great group member, he was a great solo. This was proven even after the Beatles parted ways. While they were highly successful as a group, Paul went on to have an equally as great career as a solo artist later on. Selling more than 15million records as a solo artist. Michael Jordan was great before putting on a Bulls jersey. Sure, he excelled each time he was on that court, but his independent greatness shined even brighter off the court. You can see it in all of his other business successes, including building a Jordan brand that is phenomenal. His shoes along with his clothing has gone on to become a billion-dollar empire. As for Steve jobs, well let's just say, the IPad or IPhone that you use to conduct your business would have never come to be, had Steve never realized his greatness and then ran after it.

Same is true with you. You are great all by yourself! Even before the friendship, partnership, or relationship, you are great! In fact, your security in your greatness is what's going to make your connection with other individuals so powerful. Learning your greatness, means you have learned all that you bring to the table. You know what you have to offer. And in knowing what you have to offer, it creates a standard that won't let you settle for less. Meaning, if you know that you offer loyalty in a relationship, you'll now be less likely to tolerate infidelity from a partner. When you know you are great, you behave in greatness, and you expect greatness in ever capacity.

You have to use this alone time to unlock your greatness. People settle for mediocrity, and scraps when they don't realize how great they are. Beautiful women settle for dead beat men, when they are blind to their greatness. I had a best friend who suffer in an abusive relationship and lose her life because she never located her greatness. I constantly spoke to her about her greatness, and about how she was too great to settle for such a loser; but she, herself, was unsure of this truth. And because of it she stayed and the end result was terrible. Inside that I learned something: *no one can help you own your greatness, you have to claim it for yourself.* While I was telling her how great she was, she failed to believe it for herself. And until a person claims their own greatness, they'll continue to settle for less.

    Not knowing your greatness will also cause you to cozy into something that is too small. There is nothing worse than to walk around in a pair of shoes that you've outgrown. A good friend of mine worked for a company; and in the beginning things were awesome. He was making good money, he was constantly getting promotions, and he was really advancing the company as a whole. Then, he realized that he had reached his ceiling. All of a sudden, sunny days weren't so sunny. He wasn't as enthusiastic as he once was in the office. He realized that his greatness had grown him to a point where the company he was working for was too small to nourish his growing greatness. So, my friend had to make a choice, he could either: stay and have his greatness be stunted, or he could go on and become the entrepreneur his greatness has risen to become. Needless to say, he went with his greatness, and now he is happier than ever as his own boss, working to shape and grow other great individuals, just like himself.

What is stunting your greatness? Is it small thinking? A small self-image? Bad self-talks? Nonsense activities and habit? Have you set goals for greatness? What is stopping you from the exposure of your greatness? No one is great overnight.

Greatness is a choice. Greatness is a commitment. Greatness has to be permitted. Will you permit yourself to be great?

Before you can be a great wife, master being a great woman. Before you can be a great father, master being a great man. Before you master being a great friend, master being friendly. Greatness attracts greatness. If you want to be surrounded with great people, you must initiate the process by being a great person.

LANE CHANGE: *A great "we", starts with a great "me."*

Chapter 5

Alone is designed by God

One powerful truth that I have discovered about being alone is that it is a divine place of God. Being alone is not just a status; nor just a social state of being; but it is a place. It is powerful for us to know this because, often times God will lead you to the place of alone. And you must know that when God calls you to the place of alone, it is because he wants to do something exclusive and that is just for you. Without knowing this truth, one can see being alone as trouble, instead of a teacher. Yes, your being alone is meant to be a teacher. You being alone, was on purpose; to help you realize your purpose. It was not meant to trouble you, but to teach you of all God wants to do with you.

God is always bumping and nudging you into your purpose. And your arrival into the place of alone, is God pulling you away from the crowd, away from the opinions, away from the misconceptions and misunderstandings, and he is putting you into a place where he can get you by yourself and introduce you to yourself.

LANE CHANGE: God has always used the place of alone, as the arena of introduction.

In scripture, we see that the first human created was created alone. He was not created with a partner. He was not created with a buddy. He was not created with an entourage. He was created alone. He was created alone because God needed him to understand his purpose for living, without interruption. He didn't want the man distracted with what others concluded his purpose to be. He didn't want the man distracted by what his situation and circumstances concluded his purpose to be. God kept the man alone, while he gave him the full understanding of who he was, and all that he was created to do.

Friends, this is exactly what God is doing with you. Understand, you will never get your life's purpose from anyone but God. He is the one that created you and he knows the reason behind your creation. While we often find ourselves seeking the opinion of others and getting their thought on what we should do with our lives, and who we should date, and what job we should accept, I want you to fully understand that these are all accounts that no one can provide wisdom for, but God. While you have many people in your life that want the best for you, and love you, they cannot give you the answers for your life's purpose. They are still trying to figure their own life and purpose out, so there is no way they can draw conclusion on yours. And this is why it is imperative that you allow God the opportunity to get you alone to teach you your purpose and give you direction for your life.

There are so many wonderful aspects about you that you have yet to become familiar with. There are gifts that you haven't used. Skills and talents yet to be exposed. Strengths and weaknesses that beg for your acknowledgement. The more familiar that you become with yourself the better you become. In addition, the more aware you become about yourself, the less complicated your life is. For things are only complicated, when there is ignorance. When you are blind to how a thing works, you find yourself running into many complications. And in efforts to eradicate complications, you start a cycle of trial and error to uncover how to work that thing properly.

Many have gone through trial and error to find themselves. They are unaware of their purpose, and because of it they try a multitude of things in hopes to figure it all out. They take on different jobs. They date diverse people. They adopt various religions. They move from city to city. They do good, then turn around and do bad. Trial and error! They engage in all sorts of activities, just to find themselves. And after all, they are left just as confused as when they started. Why? Because the authentic answers for all of your life's questions lie in the mind of the one who authored your life.

I call him God; but whatever you choose to call your creator or maker is up to you. However, if you are ever going to find out why you have that hot temper. Why you cry so easily. Why you were abandoned by your parents. Why you went through the divorce. Why you were brought up in the family and neighborhood you were raised in. And how it all was for the benefit of your purpose. You are going to have to go to the source.

A place I will show you

In scripture, there was a man named Abram; And God told Abram "leave your home, leave your town, leave all that you understand and are familiar with, and go to a place that I will show you. And when you arrive I will bless you." And God did just that. Abram was obedient in following God, and trusting him, and when he allowed God to lead him he was truly blessed. This is what God wants to do with you.

He is calling you to a place of blessing. And that place is called alone. God is saying come away from the dating scene for a while. Come from amongst friends. Take time away from relatives. And go to the place called alone. God is going to bless you when you arrive. There is a better woman inside you. There is a better man inside you. There is a better parent inside you. God wants to share things with you that will blow your mind. He wants to give you his plan for your life. He wants to share with you all that he intends to do. But the only way you can access this wisdom is by spending time with him.

Sometimes God will even pull people away from you to get you alone. Yes, God will ask you for alone time; but sometimes he'll create alone time himself. God is very wise, and he knows that sometimes we can be hardheaded, and won't spend that alone time that is required for us to gain awareness. And because he loves us so much, and he doesn't want us to parish in misunderstanding, he will drive people away from us to get us alone. This is why the person walked out of your life. This is why the job laid you off. This is why you and your friend separated. This was God pulling those things/people away, to get you alone. While the separation may have hurt, the introduction of yourself, makes it all worth it.

The departure of them, taught you that you could make it on your own. The lay-off from that job, freed you to be the entrepreneur you felt on the inside. See, you thought that the rain was meant to drown you, but God was causing the rain to grow you into awareness of your true self. God needs you to understand how great you are, because once you understand that you are great, you will behave in that manner. The reason people carry on in mediocrity, and accept mediocre conditions, is because they have not been exposed to their greatness.

The Fight of a Champion

"And Jacob was left alone, and a Man wrestled with him until daybreak" -Genesis 32:24

I am reminded of a man in scripture named Jacob. One day Jacob took his family off to a certain place, and he came back to his home to be alone with God. And scripture says he wrestled with God all night long. And when daytime came, Jacob refused to let God go until he blessed him. And after seeing that Jacob was sincere with his pursuit for more, God blessed him, and changed his name from Jacob to Israel. Now I am not giving you a bible lesson; However, I am talking to you about your identity.

Jacob was like you and I. He knew that there was something more to his life than what he had experienced. He knew that there was more calling. He knew he wasn't born to just work a job, pay bills, and die. He knew that life was more than arguments, despair, and confusion. He believed there was more to life than heartbreak, disappointments, and let downs. Jacob wanted more, and he refused to settle for anything less. He did what I had to do, and what I am encouraging you to do. He made alone time for he and God. He knew that the only person that could supply answers to all of his life's questions was God.

The scriptures say, "He wrestled with God." This wasn't a physical battle. This was a battle of identity and self-discovery. Have you ever had a battle with God? Have you ever wrestled with him about what you should or shouldn't do? He says "stay single", but you rather date. He says "you're not ready", but you say "Lord, I've been ready". He says "I had to take you through the foster home", and you struggle to find cause or reason why. He says "he's not the one", and you say "but God I love him." He says "you have to let her go", and you say "but God I've been with her for years." There are so many things that God does that we literally wrestle to understand. Jacob was no different. There were things that went on in his life that he needed answers to, and he locked himself up alone, in the presence of God to find out the truth. Jacob knew that the truth about his life, would make him free from all the complications in his life.

Jacob wrestled with God for a very long time. This was spelling out to us that, some of the things that God will clarify for us about ourselves will take time and patience to get a full understanding. He won't tell you everything all in one hour. You have to be willing to be alone with God for as long as it takes to get understanding. And honestly that is something that not a lot of people are willing to do. They have God on a time schedule. They give God a set time, and when he doesn't respond in that time frame, they take matters into their own hands. This is never good. But Jacob was wise enough to wait on God.

The scripture goes on to say that after God saw that Jacob was sincere and refused to leave his presence without a blessing, so God renames Jacob, Israel. This is powerful! This is exactly what God wants to do for you. He wants you to spend time alone with him so he can bless you with a name change. Up until this point you have been labeled a failure. But God wants to show you how all of your failures have trained you to release the champion inside you. Your name is about to be changed from failure to champion. Up until this point you have been viewed as worthless. But God wants to show you how he hid you long enough to prepare you to reign as the wonderful person you are. Your name is about to be changed from worthless to priceless. For some of you, you have been told "you're only a single mother." But God wants to expose the "wife" inside you. Name change! For some of you, you have been considering yourself a loser, but God wants to reveal how much of a winner you really are. Name change! For some of you your circumstances tried to name you poor, but God is about to put you in a position to be called the rich. Name Change! For others, your habits and bad choices have labeled you addict, ex con, offender. There is a name change that is about to hit your life. You are about to get your true identity. And it all comes from spending time with the true and living God.

Exclusive Revelations

God is about to share, in your alone time, some wonderful things about you. He is about to expose all of his plans and all of his intentions. He is about to give you wisdom on how you are to accomplish you dreams. He is about to speak to you about your friendships. He is about to provide the "who", and "when" about dating. He is really about to enrich your life with his great wisdom. A marvelous thing is about to occur in your alone time with God.

Now as you get this truth, you have to understand that another reason God calls you to be alone when he shares this wisdom is due to the fact that not everyone can handle what God wants to do in your life. Some people can't handle seeing you successful. Some people want to see you in lack, and in struggle. And for this cause, God pulls you away to talk to you about your past, present, and future in private. God is dedicated to giving you wholeness. And he is not going to allow anything or anyone to delay that. Notice the term "delay". No one can stop you from spending time alone with God and gaining his revelation on your life. But if you are not careful they can delay this discovery.

You must not fall into delay of getting alone with God, and understanding who you are. You can identify delay factors very easily. If a person talks against you praying or attending church, they are a delay factor. If a person is forcing you to get back out and date, versus waiting on the approval of God, they are a delay factor. If a person is occupying your attention with activities, conversation, and ideas of nothingness, they are delay factor. If a person is suggesting to you that there is no way you can have, do, or become more, they are a delay factor. If social media, and television are taking up all of your alone time, these things are also delay factors. Anything/anyone that pulls you away from spending time alone with God, to find out more about yourself, as well as him, is a factor that delays you from your purpose and chance to become all-one.

Aside from the delay factors, this exclusive time alone with God, gives you the opportunity to share things with God that others wouldn't understand. Things that may be embarrassing. Challenging. Or uncomfortable. This makes me think of my childhood, and how I was in school. Growing up I was very shy and quiet, and when I wanted to speak with my teacher about something that I didn't understand, I would wait until after class. I would wait until all the other students left and it was just me and the teacher. I did this because I didn't want to look stupid. I didn't want to be judged for what I didn't know.

I figured if I waited until we were alone, I was free to ask all the questions I wished without ridicule.

While it is not wise to care what others think about us, it's still the elephant in the room. However, that elephant gets escorted out of the room the moment you isolate yourself with God. Your alone time with God, allows you the private opportunity to be vulnerable, sensitive, and open with God, in a way that you can't accompanied by others. Not only is there exclusive revelation released from God to you, but there is, also, an atmosphere of freedom that comes along with this time of oneness with your creator.

Urgency for Discovery

You cannot wait another moment to discover your true identity, and all that you were created to have, be, and do. Your life depends on your alone time with God to learn your destiny. In addition, it is extremely important for you to realize that your discovery is not just for you, but for so many others. Yes, someone, somewhere is waiting for you to get into position. You have no idea how many people you can change and help just by walking in your purpose. Your walking in your purpose encourages others too walk in theirs. Walking out our purpose in life, requires much faith and boldness, but once we see someone else living their purpose, it strengthens us to take a leap into our own destiny. I always knew that God had created me for more than I was experiencing; However, I was terrified to step into it. I had never seen anyone in my life ever do it. Then, I begin to study the lives of some men that inspired me, and changed my life forever. People like Dr. Creflo Dollar, Pastor I.V. Hilliard, Steve Harvey, Tyler Perry, and Bishop T.D Jakes. These men, all in different ways, have ignited the courage in me to dream big, and chase after my destiny. And it was all accomplished by them being bold enough to walk in their own.

This is exactly what I am attempting to do with living my purpose. I want to inspire and motivate as many as I can to dream bigger, live bolder, and push harder toward the life they are created to lead. This is why I have put into practice everything that I am sharing with you in this book. I want my life to be an idea for others to ponder as well. I want to live so great, that it creates a desire in others to do the same. I believe this is what real leaders do. They don't dictate, they motivate. They don't tell you why your dreams can't be realized; they live a life that proves they can. And friend, this is the same for you. You are a leader, assigned by God, to lead others to their greatness and destiny. But guess what? It begins with you. There are so many people watching you, and you may not even know it. There is someone in the crowd that admires you. Someone in the corner that idolizes you. Someone in the back, in the dark, waiting for you to reach your destiny. Again, there is someone, somewhere waiting for you to get into your rightful position. They need you to succeed. It teaches them that they can too. You can't afford to waste another moment.

Chapter 6

YOU CAN'T GIVE ME WHAT I ALREADY HAVE

There is such a magnitude of blessings that come from spending time alone, and reaching the place of becoming all-one. Once you have developed from a state of being alone, into a place of being all-one, you have, now, reached a place of wholeness and independence. This is powerful. Why? Because now you are reaching a point where you are ready to welcome the company of another.

Love MUST BE Understood

Love is a powerful thing. Love can inspire. Love can uplift. Love can bring out the very best in a person. But then love can be demanding. Love can be confusing. Love can turn a person inside out. Love can make you do a whole sort of things, some of which you never thought you'd do. Before I got married. And before I became a Pastor and relationship specialist, I often wondered how something so romantic, and something so admirable such as love, could cause a person to manifest into such a dark being.

How do you go from holding hands, to later taking those same hands and abusing your partner? How do you go from saying, "I don't want to live without you" to making threats of "if I can't have you, no one can?" How does love start out so wonderful, and shift to something so traumatic? Then, the revelation came. Some love stories go from good to bad. They go from a fairytale into a horror story. Yet other love stories feature people that fall in love, and the love, like wine, gets better with time. Then, another light came on. But this time in the form of another question. What makes the two scenarios different? How could one couple go from good to bad, but another couple go from good to great? Then, it hit me. The difference is understanding.

Please understand I am an advocate for love, romance, and relationships. I think love and romance is beautiful. I think that there is nothing more wonderful than the romance and love shared between two people. I teach love. I counsel love. I promote love. And I am in love.

LANE CHANGE: In order for a thing to work properly and have great success, it must be understood. This includes love.

The number one thing that must be understood about love is it starts with you first. The reason I think many people struggle at love, relationships, and marriage is because they fail at the initial stage of it all. The stage of loving themselves. For you cannot successfully love another until you have mastered loving yourself. In fact, I believe that the prerequisite to loving another person, is loving yourself. Learning to love yourself, prepares you for loving someone else. And your love for another person should be an extension of the love for yourself. This is something I believe many people overlook. And they try to give to someone else, something, they failed at providing for themselves. But how can you successfully feed me when you are starving? How can you give me something that you have denied yourself? You can't. You can't love me, and hate yourself at the same time. You can't celebrate and encourage me, when you constantly are beating up on yourself. This is impossible. But yet, it is tried by millions every single day.

LANE CHANGE: Loving yourself is the prerequisite to loving another.

What's in will always come out

If you ever want to know how someone will love you, look at how they love themselves. For the expression of their love outwardly, is a reflection of their love inwardly. If a man beats himself up mentally and/or verbally, and you decide to partner with him, please understand it won't be long before that extension of abuse finds its way to you. Out of the men that I've counseled, there has never been one that has abused his woman, and can honestly say he loves himself. Not one. Every abusive spouse, started out as an abusive single. This type of person goes from calling himself "worthless", "stupid" "idiot", etc. And when they date, their abusive behavior isn't always as obvious. But it isn't long before what is inside begins to leak outside. And now, when you partner with him, what you are doing is stepping inside of the boxing ring, where it was a battle with himself as the target, but now you have become his opponent. And all the punches, and violence he was giving himself, he now shares with you. If he can beat up on himself, what would make him pause at beating up on you?

Same is true with someone who is feeding themselves love on a regular. This is the type of person that you want to partner with. Why? Because this person can only extend to you what they have been supplying themselves. A loving partner, stems from being a loving person. When you commit to loving yourself, you are teaching yourself to be familiar with love. And love is not foreign to you. For it is when we are familiar with a thing that we grow to appreciate and understand it. It is when we are unfamiliar that we devalue a thing and mishandle it all together. Loving yourself teaches you what love is, and how love should be carried out.

LANE CHANGE: *The expression of one's love outwardly, is a reflection of one's love inwardly.*

An addition; Not an Initiation

Love should always be activated with you first. Get comfortable with loving you first. Romance you. Cherish you. Support you. Celebrate you. This way when you do meet that special someone, you are already familiar with how all this works. The way I look at it, loving yourself preheats the oven; and when you meet that special someone you are now ready to bake the meal. The problem is so many people, are trying to bake, without preheating the oven. Then, they wonder why their relationships, partnerships, and/or friendships are still cold inside. Love takes time. It can't be microwaved; it has to be carefully prepared.

Have you been preparing for love? Preparing for love doesn't mean waiting there, doing nothing. Preparing for love means getting in the position to give and receive love. Preparing for love means initiating love toward yourself, and not waiting for someone to introduce you to love. When you meet someone, or decide to partner with them, all the things that they bring to the table should be an addition, not an initiation. The first time you get flowers should not be from them, it should be from you. The first time they tell you that you're beautiful ought to be the 2nd, 3rd, or 100th time you've heard it, because you've been telling yourself. Remember the extension of love you have for another and/or receive from another stems from the love you have inside for yourself.

Let them be Anything but "Everything"

What I am saying is don't wait for someone to give you what you should already have. Don't give someone the responsibility of being your "everything." Let them be your bonus. Let them be your add-on. Let them be your extras. **Let them be your "anything", just not your "everything".** When you make a person your "everything", you become dependent on that person. And now because they are your "everything", you are not happy unless they are around. You don't have fun unless they are around. You don't have a good day unless you talk to them. You become a puppet when you make another your "everything." And that person is the puppet master pulling all your heart strings. The bible speaks of a wife as a "good thing." Not "everything." This suggest to us that God intended for us to have love, and share in love. This is a good thing! But no one should be our "everything."

I have always been a music lover, and I believe that the best music ever produced was during the Motown era. Smokie

Robinson. Diana Ross. Stevie Wonder. Marvin Gaye. Michael Jackson. And one of my all-time favorites, the Temptations. Well, one night as I was listening to some Motown hits, I stumbled across one of my favorite Temptations songs, "I Wish it would rain." I have always loved this song, but this in particular night the lyrics really took on a whole new meaning. The first verse is as follows: *"sunshine, blue skies, please go away. My girl done found another, and gone away. With her went my future, my life is filled with gloom. So day after day, I stay locked up in my room. I know to you, it might sound strange, but I wish it would rain."*

Now I have always loved this song, and I still do. But that night I realized something that I never had before, I realized that the best love songs ever written contained lyrics of one person attaching their "everything" to another person. Lyrics filled with dependency, and desperation for another. While these songs are romantic, and endearing, they still suggest the wrong message. Take this temptation song; here we have a guy expressing that his very reason for living was destroyed the moment his woman decided to be with someone else. He expressed how his future walked out, when she did. And now day after day, he locks himself up in his room, away from everything and everyone. Then, he says "it might sound strange." But it doesn't sound strange at all. This is a song that is sung all too often, by millions all across the world.

So many fall in love, and see their partners and/or friends as their "everything." They deem them as their very reason for living. They wait for them to have a good time. They wait for them to tell them that they're beautiful or special. They lose their peace when things go wrong. They don't eat. They can't sleep. They sit up waiting by the phone. Their entire day to day activity revolves around that person. And then, if things don't go as planned with that person, they are left feeling like they have no life without them. This is not a way to live. And I don't conclude it as love, it resembles more like obsession.

Now, allow me a moment to administer tough love. Please answer this, before you met them were you living? Did you have a heartbeat? I am sure you answered yes to both. Well, while you were with them, were you still living? Did you still have a heartbeat? Again, I am sure you answered yes to both. Lastly, when you separated did you lose your breath? Did your heart stop beating? Of course, not. So, there goes the whole theory of you having no life without them. Sure, life was good with them. But your life did not start with them, neither will it end without them.

I want you to walk away from this book feeling empowered. Feeling valued. And loving yourself. I don't want this to be another book you read, get excited, and then go back to life as you knew it. I want you to truly use this book as a tool that aides you in building a greater relationship with God, with yourself, and the person(s) you love. And in saying that I need you to know that no one can be your "everything". You can't even be your "everything." Neither you nor anyone else, can provide everything you need to live a fulfilled and happy life. There is only one person that I know that can be your "Everything" and his name is God.

Only God knows how you are wired. How you are cut. And how you love and receive love. Only he can provide you with the esteem, validation, and approval to conquer life's troublesome moments. Only he can motivate, inspire, and encourage you to your greatest self. And to be direct, it is God, who gave you the friend, partner, and/or spouse. You guys didn't just happen to meet; it was arranged by God. It was God presenting that person as a gift, and you as a gift to that person. The problem always comes in, however, when we value the gift more than giver.

In scripture, we see where the first man Adam, valued his wife, Eve, (the gift), more than he valued God (the giver). And because he placed the gift more highly than the giver, we see that Adam allowed the gift to come in between him and God; resulting in Adam landing himself in much trouble (To say the least). What this spells to us is, trouble always follows when we place a "limited source" in an "unlimited source" position. We as humans are limited. God, however, is unlimited. So, if you are to make anyone your "everything", let it be someone that is unlimited. When you don't your joy becomes limited. Your happiness becomes limited. Your communication becomes limited. Your excitement becomes limited. Your potential becomes limited. Your life becomes limited. Do you see the pattern?

Whenever you make a limited person your "everything", you eventually run out. But when you make God your "everything" you always run over. It is time for you to run over in peace. Run over in joy. Run over in love. Run over in confidence. Run over in passion. Run over in creativity. And the way you do this is by shifting your investment of "everything" from a person, from yourself, and over to God.

God is supposed to be your "everything." Why? Because he is the only one that can carry the "everything" title. What happens when the person you call your "everything", decides to walk away? What happens when they have a bad day? What happens when they cheat, or do something hurtful to you? Attaching your "everything" to a person is dangerous. Because again, no one is fit to carry that load but God. Only God can be "everything" you need, when you need it, and how you need it. And God is the only sure person that will never walk out of your life. While I love my partner, and I count her priceless, she is still not my "everything". She is my good thing. But not my "everything." God is my "everything." And he is my source for everything. My life, health, strength, family, etc. he is the one responsible for it. And I say all this because the same should be realized in your life.

Who woke you up today? God. Who protected you all day long? God. Who is keeping your heart from failing? God. Who makes sure your needs and desires are given? God. God is your "everything." Whether you choose to thank him for it or not, he is. While your spouse, partner, or friend is wonderful; never put them in the position of "everything." That is a God position. And when you put a person in that position it forces them to carry the responsibility of being everything you need and want at all times. And let's be honest, who can be that? We all have flaws; and we all make mistakes. And when we make someone our "everything" we leave no room for error. That means they have to perform perfectly, even though we know that's impossible. Plus, when we give someone the position of "everything" we give them power to control us emotional, socially, and mentally. We allow them to control our enthusiasm, happiness, worth, excitement, etc. No one should have this much power in your life. And when you give a person that power, you are setting yourself up for disappointment and disaster.

You cannot put a spouse or partner or friend, in a position that is made for God. The bible teaches us that "we can do nothing separate from God." But yet, many attempt to do so. Relationships, partnerships, and friendships are no different. Many set out to build teams, without the star player. Your relationship. Your friendship. Your partnership. Your company or organization is completely incapable of functioning at its highest potential separate from God. This is not to say it won't have some level of functionality or success; but in order to function at its best level, God has to be involved. Don't hide your "everything" in a man, a woman, or a thing, hide it in God.

LANE CHANGE: *At the core of you, all that you do, and all that you are connected to… must be God.*

Chapter 7

ONE PERSON SHOW

Do You

"Do you"." Do you and I am going to do me". These were the words I heard from a very angry woman as she and her boyfriend argued a couple of spaces over at another table, in a restaurant where I was having dinner. "Do you", is what she repeatedly said as she grabbed her things and headed for the exit. In embarrassment, but still at bit angry himself, her boyfriend responded saying "that's exactly what I will do, I'm going to do me." While everyone else in the restaurant were glad that the couple had left, due to the disturbance, I was glad that they were there in the first place. Not because I enjoy seeing a couple argue, but because it sparked an idea in my mind that I would like to share with you.

What does it mean to "do you?" I am glad you asked. "Do you" is a colloquialism used to tell a person to release their inhibitions. "Do you" means you are leaving a union and about to fly solo. "Do you" means you are free to do whatever you want, and the person you are separating from is free to do whatever they want. "Do you" means there is no longer anymore ties or concerns between you and another person. "Do you" is generally an announcement or suggestion of a separation.

How often have you said "I'm going to do me?" How many times have you said that and actually done it?" I am guessing for some of you, not too often. But why? What is stopping you from doing your own thing? Is it a boy/girlfriend? Is it fear of being alone? Since you are not married, what is it that is keeping you from flying solo for a while?

I ask a lot of the singles that I counsel the same question. And the overwhelming response that I get is "I am afraid." Most people say they are afraid to do them because they don't know how things will turn out on their own. Many have become accustom to always having someone around. Many are so familiar with being in a relationship, that the idea of being single is horrific. They are used to coming home to someone, even if it's the wrong someone. Used to being a "we" and not a "me." They are uncomfortably, comfortable with the arguments, disappointments, and confrontation. Somehow, they have convinced themselves that it is better to endure the conflict of being with another person; than it is to suffer the loneliness of being alone.

I can't say I don't understand this mode of thinking; because I do. On one end, you are optimistic. You put up with the stress, because you can see the potential inside your relationship. But then, on the other end, you're like "I don't know how this can work." Trust me, I am with you. I know exactly where you are coming from. We have the thoughts of walking away and trying it on our own, but the thought of things being worse, always keeps us stuck. This is true with jobs, business moves, investments, etc. But the biggest struggle is when it pertains to matters of the heart; because now you are tapping into emotions. Sure, you can walk away from an investment, because there are no feelings involved. But try walking away from the person you love. Your mouth may say "you're done", but your heart will always force you to remember the good times. The laughs. The romance. The fun. Then, you look up and you're right back in the cycle.

But ponder this for a moment: what made you consider "doing you" in the first place? There has to be a reason behind your idea for separation. Either you were tired of the arguing. You wanted to date other people. Or maybe you just needed your space. Something provoked you to entertain the idea of you doing your own thing. But whatever that idea was, your heart talked you out of it. Now consider this, what if your heart is talking you out of the thing you really should be doing?

I know that you are often suggested to follow your heart, and let your heart be your guide. Not with me. I suggest the total opposite. Following your feelings is never a good idea. I say this because your feelings are completely unstable and unreliable.

Your feelings are tossed by every wind and idea. Your feelings are modified by so many different variables. The amount of sleep you received. Whether or not you ate. The time of day. So many things can alter your feelings. You can be up and then someone says something that rubs you the wrong way; now you're all upset. You can be extremely motivated, then you get some bad news, now you're discouraged. Your feelings change moment to moment, without warning. A great mentor of mine used to say *"don't sweat negative feelings; it's just a feeling, it will pass."* This to me was powerful. Because so many people make permanent decisions on temporary feelings.

The bible even suggests to us that it is not wise to be led by our feelings. Think of all the things your feelings have misguided you on. For some of us, feelings have led us to say things we later regretted. For others, feelings have led you into staying somewhere you knew you had outgrown. And for the rest feelings have forced you into a place of compromise and stagnation because you were afraid to disappoint another person. Whether your feelings have led you to regret, compulsion, or the appeasement of another person, you cannot afford to continue letting your feeling call the shots. It is time you walk in faith. Walk in wisdom. And walk in the direction that will provide access to your life's purpose. It is time to "do you".

LANE CHANGE: *"Doing you" means, "doing it" without them.*

Build "Team You"

Making this choice to "do you" is a full commitment. This means you are, for once, choosing yourself over other people. While this may be very difficult, it is not impossible. Understand choosing yourself, does not make you mean, hateful, or inconsiderate. It makes you strong, wise, and it puts you in a position to be better for yourself, and others later on. So, this decision must be carried out boldly, unapologetically, and without restriction. Take this opportunity and time to walk in freedom. Be free to truly do all the things you've always wanted but never were afforded the privilege.

Allow yourself the moment to invest in yourself. It's all about "team you" right now. Do me a favor, say: "I support team me." This is what you have to remind yourself throughout this process. Because often you are going to feel the urge to seek company. You are going to experience urges to depart from the process. But you have to remember you are doing this for the empowerment of "team you."

"Team you" is major. There are dreams inside "team you". Goals inside "team you". Vision inside "team you". A great career inside "team you." "Team you" is an empire of greatness waiting to be manifested. I encourage you to dream big, pray about them, and then run after them with all that you have.

I also encourage you, in this time, to travel the world. Go outside your hometown. God created more than just the city you live in. Go explore the world. The way I look at it, you are single so it won't cost you as much money. Go! Meet new people. Learn new languages. Take up new hobbies. Try out living in another part of the world. And if it doesn't work out, come on back. Take advantage of this freedom!

The last thing you want is to trade in your freedom for frustration. So many people miss the opportunity in their singleness to maximize their freedom; and they get into relationships and marriages, and become frustrated. They become frustrated when they look back on all the things they should've, could've, and would've did, had they had done what I am suggesting to you.

LANE CHANGE: *A little separation anxiety now, beats a load of regret later.*

The Gift of Selfishness

The reason I am pushing so hard for you to build and do you is because you are in a golden moment. When you are single, you have the elite privilege to invest entirely in yourself without having to feel guilty. You don't owe anyone anything. You don't owe an explanation. You don't need permission. You don't have a curfew. You don't even have to make an announcement. You are free to come, go, do, and build as you please. This is a freedom that you won't always have, so why not maximize on it?

Soon you will enter a relationship or marriage and this freedom will be altered. If you don't have them already, soon children will come along and this freedom will be altered. Your singleness affords you a freedom to be selfish. Now in partnership, relationship, friendships, or any other union selfishness is frowned upon. Selfishness is unwelcomed. Why? Because you can't successfully partner with another person, expecting the union to work, and one or both people are selfish. Selfishness can destroy any type of partnership or relationship.

However, while selfishness is poison in a relationship; it is powerful in singleness. Singleness allots you space to do everything you desire without consideration. There is no one else to consider. You can eat what you want, without debate. Watch what you want on television, without an argument. Whatever you desire, you are free to do it. It is all about self, when you are single. As long as what you do is legal, morally correct, and you can still look yourself in the mirror and be content, go for it. Get all your selfish habits and behaviors out, because once you enter a relationship or marriage, you are committed to a life of compromise and selflessness.

LANE CHANGE: The reason many people are selfish in relationships is because when they were single, they never took time to sow their selfish oats.

Dinner party of one

Man, I tell you there is nothing like going out and having a good time with family and friends. The laughter. The stories. The jokes. Some of my fondest moments were when I was out with my loved ones. I am sure you can attest to this yourself. But for a moment I want to present you with a challenge. Now I say challenge because not all of you will be willing to go through with this. I have challenged many singles with this and the feedback has been unanimous, for those that actually carried the challenge out. They all agree that this challenge was life changing.

I challenge you to date yourself. Sounds silly, right? I know. But no matter how silly it sounds, that's the challenge. I want you to set a date and time, get all dressed up, and go on a wonderful date with yourself. Because the idea of dating yourself seems silly, certain singles refuse the idea entirely. They wouldn't be caught dead dating themselves. But these are the individuals that miss out on the opportunity to truly change their perspective on being single.

Who said you had to wait on another person to go see a movie? You want to see it; so, go see it. Who said you needed company to enjoy a nice meal? Make the reservation, and go enjoy the dinner. For the longest, you've consider a great time to be between two or more people. Well it still can be a great time. And it still can be two or more people. Book the dinner for a party of one; but three people will show up. And their names are "me", "myself", and "I." Seeing as though you all have so much in common; I promise you, the three of you all will have a blast. You can laugh. Tell jokes. Go to a play. Go bowling. Take a trip. You name it! There is no limit to the fun you can have with just me, myself, and I.

While many are up for the challenge; there are some that are wrestling with questions. "Won't I look weird?" "Won't people laugh at me?" "Am I that pathetic?" Oh no. On the contrary, you are not pathetic at all. It is bold, and a sure sign of security to go out and enjoy a great time by yourself. No one will laugh at you. Except maybe those that are too insecure to try it themselves. And as far as looking weird, what's weird about it? I have found that the reason many don't take the time to date themselves is for two reasons. One, they never thought about it. And two, they over thought about it, and all the embarrassing thoughts talked them out of it.

Let's settle this. There is nothing wrong with being good to yourself. There is nothing wrong with dating yourself. And there is nothing wrong with spoiling yourself. There is actual a lot to gain in dating yourself.

a) **An Extension of Self Love.** Remember the prerequisite to loving someone else properly is to love yourself properly. Doing nice things for yourself in private is one thing, but when you choose to go public, it takes on a whole new meaning. Just like with dating another person. Sure, you are willing to date them; but until they are willing to make it public, there is no real validity behind it. They can say how they feel in private all day long, but it is what they are willing to declare publicly that provides the stamp of authenticity. What makes your love any different? Nothing. You can walk around and profess that you love yourself all you want, but where is the proof? What signs do you have? Display your love. Send yourself some flowers. Buy yourself a gift. Wine and dine yourself. And don't be cheap. You are expressing your love toward yourself. Don't wait for someone to come along and show you a good time. Create your own experience.

b) **Dating Awareness.** Providing this type of experience not only gets you familiar with being loved on, and in the habit of treating yourself; but it also, teaches you things about yourself that you didn't know. And makes you better aware of how you would like to be treated by another. When we are dating, we teach others how to treat and love us; but when we are single, we, ourselves, are learning how we want to be treated and loved. We cannot teach others to do what we have not mastered. Find out what you like to do for fun. Find out what excites you. Find out things that you think are romantic. The worse thing in the world, is to try to love someone, who doesn't know how they like to be loved.

c) **Learn the Hot spots.** By going out, and going out often it gives you a chance to find great date locations. This is essential for enhancing your dating experience. So, when you begin to date yourself go to a wide range of locations. And don't be cheap with yourself. Go to the best of the best places. Spend a little extra, you're more than worth it. Besides it's unfair to demand another to take you somewhere and/or spend what you are unwilling to for yourself.

Learn the places you had the most fun. Learn the places that had the best food. Learn the places that were awesome alone, but could be better with a partner. Then, when you're asked on a date and where you would like to go, you will have the perfect place because you've already taken yourself there.

You go alone first, have a good time, and when you go back with a friend or date, your good time becomes a great time. At least it is supposed to. If you have a better time alone at a place, than you did with the company of another, you have to pay attention to this. The fact that you had a better time alone than you did with them may be a sign that they are not company you should continue to keep. When you involve another party on your dating experience, the fun and excitement you had solo ought to be doubled now that you went there as a couple.

d) **Self-affection ignites the affection of another.** Loving yourself in this fashion is something that is visible; and your self-affection can be seen by others. This includes potential daters. Many people are interested in you, but don't know how to approach you. So, what they do is admire you from a distance. They do so with hopes that you provide clues on how they can get next to you. What are you showing them? What conclusions do they get when they see you loving yourself? Do they conclude you to be an easy win? Or do they see you as a high hanging fruit that one must be willing to climb to behold?

LANE CHANGE: The way you are treating yourself teaches others to come along and follow suit.

Chapter 8

The Standards of Singleness

I am a huge fan of watches. In fact, I have been collecting watches for many years. My love for watches is never ending. I love all types of watches. Sports watches. Aviator watches. Luxury watches. Diamond watches. Mechanical watches. Any type of watch you can name, I have some level of admiration for it.

      I can recall some time ago, I entered a watch store, with hopes of purchasing a nice watch for a friend. Now when I walked into the store, I noticed that some watches were displayed out in the open around the store; while other watches rested inside locked glass cases along the walls of the store. The ones that were out in the open were accessible to everyone. Any man, woman, or child that wanted a closer look at the watches had their opportunity. There was nothing prohibiting the watches from being touched, dropped, damaged, or stolen. Some of these watches even had a big, red sign above them that read "clearance." Meaning that the price of the watches had been discounted and marked down. While I had no attraction to the any of the watches out on the floor, I still recall looking them over. And let me tell you, the watches that were out in the open weren't enticing at all. They were skimpy. Flawed. Dusty. Partially Scratched. Ugly. They had very little, to no value at all. The only thing that was appealing about these watches was that they were extremely cheap. The store owner couldn't care less about those watches. And having seen them, I understood.

    Then, I took my attention over to the watches that laid away in the locked glass cases along the walls. These watches were beautiful. They were clothed in white gold. Classic gold. Platinum. They were endowed with rubies. Emeralds. Diamonds. These watches were very easy to look at. But not only were they expensive in quality and appeal; they were expensive in price. This explained why they were locked away. These watches were such high quality that the store owner felt the need to keep them secluded. Protected. Guarded. And while they were locked away, they were still able to be seen and admired. You could see them, but you couldn't touch them. Unlike the less admirable watches, these were not accessible to everyone. You had to seek assistance to behold these watches. These watches were held to such a standard that they demanded respect.

What type of "watch" are you?

Why did I notice all of this? Why did any of this observation matter to me? I had no clue until I was driving home from the jewelry store, and I heard the voice of God pose a question to me. He had asked, very plainly, "What type of watch are you?" Then, it hit me. Every day that we live, and in all that we do, there is someone watching us. Some in the shadows. Someone in the back. Someone that we never would suspect. There is someone watching us at all times. Whether it be a child, spouse, friend, or stranger. You are playing the role of a watch for somebody. The question remains "what type of watch are we?" Now when I was posed this question it really made me think; and because it was posed by God, I knew I had to be honest. But before I could answer, God interrupted my gathering of thoughts, and gave me an assignment. And that assignment was to pose the same question to you.

Now you wear many different hats; and you perform many diverse roles. You have to admit that you are in high demand from others. But I have to let you know that while you are carrying out your duties, and living your life day by day, the number one role that you perform is of a watch. You are on watch by someone at every moment. When you go to work. When you are at the mall. While you are grocery shopping. While you simply walk from your car to your house. You are performing as a watch. And the question that the Lord wanted me to ask you is "what type of watch are you?" What is it that people see when they watch you? What image are you portraying? Do you shine with confidence? Do you shimmer with grace? Or are you damaged with insecurities? Scratched with arrogance? What type of watch are you? This is something that forces you to be open and honest.

Are you a watch that is discounted, cheap, and accessible to everyone? Or are you a watch that is expensive, radiant, and deserving to be placed on the highest shelf? People may never say a word to you. They may never even give you an idea that they are watching you. But they are. And they will treat you just as they see you.

Value births Respect

The level of respect a person gives is always based on the value. If no value is seen, no respect is produced. You will never see a person skipping diamonds across a pond, as they would a rock. Why? Because the diamond holds too much value, to be just thrown around like a rock. When a person sees value, they immediately submit respect. Are people watching value when they see you? Or are they just watching another person behaving worthlessly? If you are not receiving the respect that you desire, it could be that you have been displaying the wrong images.

Growing up I often heard if you want respect you have to give it. Well, I have to disagree with that statement. A bear has never respected me, but I respect it. A lion has never respected me, but I respect it. A snake has never respected me, but you better believe I have much respect for it. While it sounds nice to put a sowing and reaping spin on respect; it is just not true. Just as the bear, lion, and snake, did nothing to earn respect; you don't have to contribute anything to earn the respect of anyone either.

LANE CHANGE: *To gain the respect of another is to simply show yourself deserving of respect.*

I respect the bear, lion, and snake because when I watch them, I can clearly see their power and abilities. I see their strengths. I notice their killer instincts. I can see that if not respect and regarded, these animals can be very big problems for me. I have watched them long enough to develop a respect for them.

What prejudice and/or conclusions are people making having watched you? Are they concluding that you are timid? Weak? Bold? Assertive? What have people noticed about you? There are some people that I value and respect highly, and I have never even met them. But my identification of their value has given birth to the great respect that I have for them. I am sure you have people that you respect in this same manner. And my goal is for you to become so aware of the images you are displaying that you, yourself, become an icon that many people openly and privately grow to respect in the highest regards. The key to raising your level of respect is to first raise your level of value.

Appeal Value:

What does your attire say about you? Does it suggest that you don't care? Does it suggest that you are easy? Are you showing what you should be saving? Your attire is a part of your appeal. Your appeal is what people see when they see you. They may never speak to you, but they will see you; and you want to speak volumes. You are a walking billboard. You are an advertisement in motion. And you must be sure that you are marketing the right things.

LANE CHANGE: Whatever you market, you are going to attract those types of buyers.

If you market body parts, you will get the attention of those seeking body parts. But if you market your intelligence, and self-respect, you will grasp the attention of those that wish to respect you in that same manner.

Same is true if you market friendliness. The bible teaches us to show ourselves friendly if we want to attract friends. Real friends are only attracted to authentic friendliness. And the reason many attract backstabbers, and friend impersonators is because they displayed such an image. A wise man once said "don't dress like where you are, dress like where you want to be." Now I am not suggesting that you go broke trying to buy the latest and most expensive fashion. What I am saying is make a statement in your appearance. Look like a person going somewhere. Look like a person ready to conquer the world. It's time to appeal to the company you wish to keep. It's time to look like the "you" that you aspire to become.

Vocal Value:

The scripture teaches us that the power of life and death is in our tongues. This means that every time you open your mouth, you are either killing a thing or giving life to a thing. Have you been using your mouth as a weapon to commit your own suicide? Or have you been living off the resuscitation of your words? Every time you open your mouth you are either causing someone to respect you more, or to respect you less. One of my pet peeves is to see a beautiful woman, with a vulgar vocabulary. I think that is the fastest way to make a beautiful woman turn ugly. I don't even have to be speaking to them personally; I could just be around them and immediately I become annoyed by their foul language.

Are people being turned off by your poor vocabulary? What person have you inspired just because they heard you speak? Remember every time you speak you are either killing respect, or giving birth to it.

I believe the way a person speaks tells you what type of person they are. If you ever want to find out what type of person you are entertaining, don't waste your time asking them a bunch of questions; just sit quiet and listen to them speak. Soon they will reveal everything you need to know. The scripture goes on to say that "out of the abundance of the heart the mouth speaks." What this means is the true intentions of a person's heart will always be revealed by the words they speak. If a person doesn't have any respect for you, eventually they will say something that identifies their lack of respect. If a person honors you, soon you be informed by the flattery of their words. Listen to the way a person speaks to and about you, and it will announce their level of value for you.

However, while you are listening to their words, I want you to take note of the words that you speak as well. The way you speak is an audible reflection of your inward mindset and self-image. We as people speak from inward perception. Take a person who is always using profanity. They use profanity because they see it as powerful. They curse to make their point more dramatic. They curse to show that they mean what they say. But profanity only proves how much power they actually don't have. A person of great influence and power has a vocabulary that is empty of profanity. They don't have to curse to display their passion. Neither do they have to be demeaning in their talking to make themselves seem superior.

> **LANE CHANGE:** *When you take inventory of your vocabulary, you expose what is being harbored in your heart.*

Now judging by your language and choice of speech, what types of images has your heart become a house for? Have you been speaking loneliness? Regret? Jealousy? Mediocrity? Or have you been providing shelter for love? Honor? Elegance? And decency? Whatever you have been speaking out of your mouth is the thing that you are giving life to. And that is the very thing that others will come along and support. So, start talking better, bigger, and on purpose.

You have the power to speak a thing into existence. Your words carry the power of attraction. You speak defeat, and defeat will come from all directions. Likewise, you speak promotion and you will soar to higher heights. You speak in disrespectful phrases and words, and it will welcome all things disrespectful. Your lack of respect in words, teaches others to respond to you in disrespectful words.

For instance, I don't know when it ever became cool for woman to refer to each other as the "B" word. In my opinion, it has never been seen as cool. It has always been a term of disrespect. But for some reason the term has become more and more acceptable. Woman are strutting around saying "I'm a bad B-word" "I'm a fine B-word" "I'm an independent B-word". Many women have neglected from being a queen, and have settle with being the queen "B". This is unacceptable. It used to be a time where women would get mad when anyone would call them the "B-word"; but now some women have found a way to turn it into a term of endearment.

This is no different than racist, sexist, or religious slurs that are spoken on a regular. When disrespectful words are seen flowing from your mouth, it spells that you accept and support it. So, others, like a boomerang, send that same type of disrespect back to you.

> *LANE CHANGE: Is it disrespect when someone else degrades you, after hearing you degrade yourself? Or is it called "speaking your language"?*

Behavioral Value:

How are you carrying yourself? Are you masquerading around like a person going nowhere fast? Or are you walking like a person with a purpose? Are you seen as a pile of pity? Or do you stand tall, like a statue of greatness? There is a reason people respect the president. There is a reason people respect doctors. There is a reason people respect soldiers. Because they carry themselves with dignity. Their behavior demands respect. Their actions draw in admiration like a magnet. They don't have to go out of their way to earn honor, they simply commit to honorable deeds, and the respect follows.

What actions have you been committing to? In my relationship, we always say "don't show me your commitment in words, show me in your actions." So often people profess to be committed to a thing or person, but their actions display the complete opposite.

Many say they don't care what people think, yet their behavior cries so loudly for acceptance and approval from others. Many say they respect themselves, but then you see these same individuals half naked on social media. The same person you hear screaming "I'm responsible", most times is the same person you see behaving wildly and landing themselves in prison, for nonsense. So many people make declarations, but their behavior exposes their lack of commitment to the thing they declared.

In communication, most of what you say to another person is not coming out of your mouth, it is coming out of your body language or your behavior. Studies show that communication is broken into three parts: tone (38%), words (7%), and body language (55%). As you can see it is what we express through our body language and behavior that conveys the majority of what we are communicating.

What value is your behavior adding? People will often see you and treat you the way you act. Your actions give them the green light to act the same way towards you. If you are seen degrading yourself, they will consider it acceptable to come along and give assistance with the degrading activity. Never forget people that come into our life, come to assist us with whatever is already taking place. If you celebrate yourself, they will come and be your biggest cheerleader. If you are neglecting or downing yourself, they will come along and show you how it's really done.

Many people use your actions to shine wisdom on what they can get away with. If you are behaving like a person that depends on the acceptance of others, many will play on that and use it as a way to control you. If you behave as if you are a prisoner of your situation and like nothing good will ever happen to you, people pick up on that. And they will give you their bare minimum of effort, because they have realized you will accept anything you can get because you don't expect anything more.

Our behavior highlights the type of behavior we condone. A person will only treat you like you allow them. If you allow disrespect, I promise, you will find an overwhelming number of people that will supply you with all the disrespect you can muster. However, if you demand respect, I guarantee that you will attract those that are willing to provide you with the supply of respect to meet your demand. It all comes with recognizing your value, and setting standards.

Standards Provide Safety

One of the biggest tragedies that I feel has plagued many generations, my generation included, is the absence of standards. If we examine social media, music, television, and even our day to day interaction with people. It is apparent that many individuals are lacking standards. They just take and run with whatever is given. There are no qualifications to get their attention. They are open to the public in every sense of the term.

I believe that standards are necessary. Not everyone is worthy of having access to you. Not everyone is qualified to handle you. Some people will damage you, scar you, or leave you all broken up. And for this cause, standards are necessary. Standards aide in your protection. Standards are like that locked glass case that protects the expensive watches in the jewelry store I visited. Without that locked glass case, these valuable, incomparable, admirable watches would have been in the same danger of the lesser watches. And due to their value, they would have been sought after first. Maybe the first to be stolen. Damaged. Dropped. But to protect the valued watches, the owner locked them away safely.

Too often we have valuable individuals behaving poorly. Making stupid decisions. Fighting like animals. Acting like criminals. Wasting countless, once in a lifetime moments.

Presenting their bodies to anyone that winks at them.

Committing to "situationships", sex buddies, and hook-ups.

LANE CHANGE:

A **situationship** is defined as being involved with another person and there is no clear goal or direction for the involvement. The two of you are just *going with the flow*. And there are no real commitments or titles.

They do all of this and much more because they have failed to set up standards. And they fail to set up standards because they are unaware of their value. Just as the knowledge of value births respect from others for you; the knowledge of value you see for yourself births standards. The moment you discover your value, that will be the moment you build standards. You don't protect a thing you don't see as valuable. Only the things you see that have great significance and rarity.

It is time that you see yourself as valuable. It is time that you see yourself as unique, special, and a rare breed. You are not the same as the person you grew up with. You are not another statistic or status quo. You are not a product; you are a person. You are a person that is marvelously and wonderfully made in the image of God. You are a person that wants and can have more out of life. You are a person that is intelligent. Beautiful. Sophisticated. And admirable, all by yourself.

You are a woman that is elegant. You are a woman that is deserving of being treated as the queen you are. You are worth more than rubies, and you shine greater than any diamond. You are amazing. And I need you to become aware of this truth.

I know you are saying but you don't even know me. I don't have to personally know you to know this truth. I know that you are made by the Lord, and the Lord doesn't make junk. Even his piece of mess is a masterpiece. You may have made some mistakes and you may have not been cared for the way you should have been, but let me inform you that you are not the mistakes you made. You are not the hurtful things that folks have labeled you. They were just too ignorant to realize your value. But I see your value. And seeing as though you are reading this book, you see it too, and you really want for your light to shine. I don't just want you to see you value. I want you to protect it. It's not enough to for you to only be aware that you are valuable; you have to make sure that others see your value and they respect it. Standards will shine awareness that you are valuable, and your standards will cover you from those who can't afford your attention, time, and energy.

Brother, you are a man built by God. You are made just like God. You are strong. Creative. Brilliant. Innovative. You are full of authority and geared with dominion. You are not a weakling. You are not timid. You are not insecure. You are a warrior. You are an icon of real strength. You weren't created to adopt the habits and nature of a thug, dope boy, or baby daddy. Those are left for the lost, and simple minded. But you were meant to shine light on what it truly means to be a man. You are a father, husband, friend, and mentor to many men that aren't afraid to ask for help. You are truly a sight to behold. And as I stated, I don't have to know you, personally, to understand this truth about you. Your purchase of this book, identifies your hunger to go beyond where you are, and into your destiny. Your quest for greatness has exposed your inward champion. And when you are a champ, you can't waste time with chumps.

Standards protect you from those that may harm you in some way. Standards serve as a burglar alarm, and they alert you when an intruder is around. You need standards to identify individuals who come to rob you of your greatness. Introducers such as fake friends, shifty spouses, jealous relatives, and dream killers. Standards help you weed out all those that don't belong in your life. And standards ensure that only those that support, encourage, and increase your value have the privilege of your attention.

Standards force you to raise the bar, and keeps you from settling. One of the worse things is to see a person with all the potential in the world, waste it by dumbing down and trying to be cool with someone who doesn't have nearly as much significance. Behaving like an idiot just to gain the attention and acceptance of people who are going nowhere. Entertaining the lies and excuses of individuals just so they don't have to be alone.

Where are the standards? Don't you know standards identify that you are worthy of honor and respect? Or is that no longer a concern? Do you no longer care how people treat you and care for you? People will only treat you the way that you allow them. If you allow disrespect they will give it. But if you demand respect, it will be a requirement. People respect standards; you just have to create some!

Know the truth, or Fall for the lie

Understanding your value results from you discovering who you are. This is why I encourage you so greatly to spend time alone to study yourself. You have to know who you are and who you are not. You have to understand that you are not your mistakes. You are not your flaws. You are not your education, neighborhood, or the money you make. Spend time learning who you really are. This is important, because if you don't learn the truth about who you are, you just may adopt a false identity. Many will come along and try to conclude who you are by their assumption, and your unawareness to who you truly are will cause you to end up settling for who they assume you to be, instead of truly living as you were created to be. How terrible it would be to live a lie, because you weren't exposed to the truth.

I Am...

An additional route to defeating the opinions and labeling of others is to develop "I AM" statements. In scripture, we discover that God is the great I AM. What that means is God is our "everything." God is our healer. Our helper. Our provider. Our protector. For all of these God says "I am." The entire earth was created and responds to God, (I Am). In fact, whenever "I am" is released from our mouths whatever follows is attracted to us. Reason being is the earth and everything in it respects God as "I Am." So, when "I am" is spoken, everything responds.

Notice how when you say "I am tired" and you seem to get even more fatigue. Notice how when you say "I am not in the mood" and everything all of a sudden begins to annoy you. This is the power of "I Am." "I Am" is a magnet for anything that follows after it. I explained all of this to you because it is time you master your "I am" statements.

LANE CHANGE: Your "I am" protects you from other people's "you are."

Many have no awareness of the attractive power of "I Am." So, they make statements loosely without ever realizing the danger. They have no clue that "I am" welcomes whatever they utter afterwards. So, they say things like "I am broke." "I am weak." "I am lonely." And then, they wonder why all of these begin to suffocate them. They are broke, weak, and lonely because they said it. Oh, how life-changing this would be if they redirected this power in the correct direction. If they started saying things like "I am rich", "I am strong", and/or "I am all-one." There is great power in the attraction of "I am."

I personally feed myself "I am" statements every morning; and I go throughout my day empowered. This is a strategy that I have taught to others, and a key that I am extending to you. The scriptures support this practice. In scripture, we find that *faith comes by hearing*. The more you hear a thing, the more you start to believe it. This is how "I AM" statements work. You repeat and announce them over your life daily; and with each day the faith you have in what you are saying begins to grow. This then, builds your confidence and self-esteem. You go from being shaky to unmovable.

However, instead of awaiting the declarations of others, we have to make declarations to ourselves. Start telling yourself who you are. Every time you speak to yourself this way, you are sowing seeds of greatness and affirmation into yourself; and no negative person will be able to distract you and pull you away from your place of greatness.

Chapter 9

Image is Everything

"Imagination is everything. It's the preview to life's coming attractions." -Albert Einstein

In the 80's there was a very popular slogan that was quoted by almost every celebrity on television. That powerful slogan consisted of three words "image is everything." This was brilliant because what that slogan revealed was that the way you perceive a thing will be the way you receive a thing. Others say it like this "perception is reality." It is how you conclude a thing in your mind that will alter how you treat or mistreat that thing. Furthermore, if you want to change the action of a person, you must first change their thinking. This is the power of image. And this power is everything.

You want to be a millionaire? Start thinking like one. You want to be a wife? Start thinking like one. This is not magic.

This is the power of imagination. And your imagination is located and operates in the confines of your mind. The scripture tells of a story about a group of people that wanted to build a tower from earth to heaven. One day, these people gathered around and said "let us build a tower that will take us up to heaven." Then, the scripture goes on to say that God looked out and saw the tower they had built. However, as I began to study the scripture and read a little more, I discovered the tower was not yet built physically; but God saw that the tower was built in their *imagination*. The scripture goes on with God saying "nothing will be impossible for them, which they have imagined to do." God was not focused on the physical, he was looking at the mindset and hearts of the people. He saw that they had already set their mind on building the tower. And because their mind was set on building the tower, nothing would be able to stop it from coming to pass.

Our imagination is the tool that we use to build our reality. If you can't see a thing in your imagination, you can never see it in your reality. I'll go even further to say that the very fact that you can see a thing in your imagination is proof that it is possible in your life.

Walt Disney saw "Disney World" in his imagination before he ever saw it in Florida. Steve Jobs saw "Apple" in his imagination before he saw it in the form of various electronics in the stores. I saw this book in my imagination before I saw it on the book shelves. Again, the ability to see a thing in our imagination proves that it can come to pass.

Even God used the tool of imagination. In scripture, God is found saying "let us make man in our own image." Image is the root word for imagination. So, what He was saying was "let us make man in our imagination." God, then, goes on to say what type of man he wanted to create, and how much dominion and power he would have. Then, once he built man in his imagination, he was able to manifest man in the physical world. He saw man in his imagination, before he saw him in the earth.

The key to your life's success is all in your imagination. Image is everything. Your image is the difference between alone and all-one. Rich and poor. Full and empty. You determine your reality by what you build in your imagination.

Start Building

How does this relate to your singleness? Well I believe the type of people we attract is all due to our imagination. Without us being fully aware of it, our perception has become our reality. But I truly believe we can change the people we attract by simply imagining on purpose. Remember, before we can ever see a thing in our life, we must see it in our imagination. So, with this in mind, we have to do as God and the people in the scripture did and build with our imagination.

Build the type of career you want. Build the type of friend you want. Build the type of house you want. Build the type of spouse you want. Do this, and the Lord promised us that nothing will keep us from having that which we build in our imagination.

When building in your imagination there are two things you want to remember. (1) **Build with the assistance of God; not just with your own desires**. This act of building in our imagination is spiritual and requires the guidance of God. Therefore, seek God on the type of spouse, friend, and partner you should be building. (2) **Build more than physical**. It is fine to desire and build a nice looking spouse; but let's build more inwardly. Because he/she can be very attractive, but not be who you need in every other area. Then, you'll find yourself in the same place you've always been. Build in your imagination someone that will respect and honor you. See yourself in a fulfilling, loving, wonderful relationship. See yourself in a supporting and devoted friendship. See yourself living your purpose. These are the things that you should be building in your imagination and meditating on.

Vision Authenticates Imagination

What you are doing is creating a vision. A vision is your life's blueprint. Your vision is how life will be once you get beyond your current moment. You may be single, but your vision draws you in a fulfilling relationship and/or marriage. You may be an employee, but your vision draws you in an amazing career living your dream. A vision is important. The scripture tells that we need a vision to live; or else we die because we stop believing we can have more.

A vision serves as a roadmap to discovery. Our vision is the checklist that we use when we meet potential friends, partners, and spouses to see if they are the one.

LANE CHANGE: Without a vision, we have nothing to authenticate that we have found the one we created in our imagination.

God built, in his imagination, the type of man he wanted in the earth. And I am telling you ladies and gentlemen that you are made in the likeness of God, with the same power he has. In addition, I am telling you just as he created the man he wanted in the earth, you have the power to build the type of spouse, partner, and friend you want in your life. Stop worrying and complaining, and start imagining and building.

Chapter 10

Let's Talk About Sex

Ok! So, let's go there. Let's talk about sex. Sex is something that will definitely come up while you are single. I wish I could tell you that there was a special pill you can take that would remove your desire for sex, but I can't. We were made to be sexual beings; so, there are going to be sexual moments that arise. However, it is my goal to help you handle sex when it comes up while you are single, and on your journey to becoming all-one.

Biblically and morally we have been taught that sex is sacred and should be reserved for marriage. This is exactly what I promote as well. Sex should be saved for the person you marry. However, while having sex only after we are married is honorable, most people struggle with this goal. In their heart, they may want to wait, but are just having a hard time carrying the commitment out. Not because they are immoral or rebellious against scripture, but because they have sexual desires and sometimes they are extremely difficult to deny.

If we'd be honest the reason that sex is so hard to deny is because it is so good. Especially with the right partner. That's just the realness about it. The problem comes with finding the right partner. I am sure we all can attest that there have been times that we've had sex, and then thought "what a waste of time". Ladies, you've said "I got all sexy for that?". And fellas you've said "man, she may be fine, but that was trash." Most of us that have been sexually active has had an experience that we wish we hadn't. For some of us we've had many experiences that we wish we hadn't.

This is exactly what I hope to help you with. Eliminating further bad sexual experiences. To be more specific, I want to help you eliminate all sexual experiences until you find the one fitting to have you. All of you. Spirit. Mind. And body.

Now we all know that there is a double standard when it comes to sex as it pertains to men and women. A man can have many sexual partners and he is deemed desirable or experienced. While a woman can have the same number of sexual partners and she is deemed loose, or used goods. Sad, but we live in a world that focuses more on what to call a man/woman that has had several sexual partners, and cares little to nothing about the effects of having several sexual partners.

However, I want to turn your attention to the truth. The truth as it relates to sex and singleness is the more sexual partners that you have the more you have to fight off spiritually.

SOUL TIES

When we are given the story of the birds and the bees we are often only given this fairytale story about when a man loves a woman, the two of them engage in sex to express their love for one another. This is where we get the term "making love". While this story is innocent, enduring, and cute. It is incorrect. When a man and a woman have sex they are not making love. There is no such thing as making love. That's just something endearing someone came up with to refer to sex. However, whenever we engage in sex something is being made, and that is a connection. This connection is called a soul tie.

A soul tie is an entwining of energies between you and the person you sleep with. The moment you and another person have sex you become connected to them mind, body, and spirit. When you have sex with a person because of soul ties, you are not only being joined with them but with every person they had sex with, and every person that person that had sex with, and so on. Your one sexual encounter with this person, connects you to a chain of other spirits. This is how you get an STD, *spiritually transmitted disease.*

PROTECT MORE THAN YOUR BODY

I understand that while we are taught about sex, we are warned about the dangers of Sexual transmitted diseases. Commonly knowns as STD. However, that is only part of the definition. While we are warned of things that affect our bodies like Chlamydia, HIV/AIDS, Syphilis, etc. We are never warned about things that can affect us beyond the body.

Regardless of what your spiritual beliefs and preferences may be, one thing that must be made clear is that while we are human beings, we are spirit beings first. We were created by God, who is a spirit. And made like God. Making us also a spirit. We are spirits that live in physical bodies. And I believe it to be extremely important that we pay more attention to our spirits than we do our bodies. For the spirit is the real you. Your body is just the vehicle used to carry you along the earth.

To make this simple, consider a fish inside of a fishbowl. The bowl is not the fish. The fish is the living thing inside the bowl. When you clean the bowl, you are not cleaning it for the sake of the bowl, but for the sake of the fish. When you put the fish bowl in a secure place, you are not securing the bowl, but you are securing the fish inside the bowl.

Beloved, you are that fish. Your body serves as the fish bowl. What good is it to protect the bowl, without protecting the fish inside? For after all, it is the fish that is the main focus. The bowl is just the living space of the fish.

The reason billions of people are spiritually infected with diseases is because they are not taught or made aware of *spiritually transmitted diseases.* So, while we protect our bodies (the fish bowl) from sexual transmitted diseases by practicing "safe" sex; our spirit self (the fish) gets attacked spiritually. This now shatters the theory of "safe sex" altogether. There is no such thing as safe sex.

You may be able to wear a condom during sex; And that condom may protect your body from unplanned pregnancies and *sexually* transmitted diseases. Even that is a 99.9% chance. But what protects your spirit self from *spiritually* transmitted diseases? Well, there has been not such protection invented to protect against spiritually transmitted diseases. The only way to protect and guard ourselves from spiritually transmitted diseases is by abstinence and celibacy. Yes, the only way to keep from getting burned is to stay away from the fire.

IS IT WORTH IT?

Sex may be good, but is it worth your peace of mind? Is it worth emotional instability? Is it worth the sexual unbalance? Because these are all the things you encounter when you have sex. Remember a soul tie is a connection with you and the person you have sex with. A collaboration of energies and feelings. So, if you meet a person that carries tons of negative energy, and you agree to have sex with them, what you are doing is giving them permission to transfer their negative energies into you.

Anger. Rage. Depression. Anxiety. Fear. Paranoia. Low-esteem thought patterns. These are some of the spiritual diseases that come with soul ties. Whatever that person is mentally, spiritually, or emotionally is what they give to you when you two have sex. Furthermore, you pack on the energies of anyone and everyone that they have ever had sex with, and vice versa.

Soul ties are nothing to take lightly. Soul ties are very real and have very real effects. Notice how no matter how many sexual partners you've had; you always remember your first sexual partner. Notice how the smallest thought can cause you to recall a sexual encounter you've had in the past. Even if the encounter was years prior. These are all due to the soul connection that you share with that person(s).

Obsession is even developed due to soul ties. This is when you have urges, desires, or the need to be a bit more clingy or dependent of the person that you've had sex with. This is found most common with women. However, men are not exempt. The reason that this craving is birthed is because you only got a part of that person you had sex with. And that small part that you now carry desires to be feed. However, it can only be feed by the same person or a person with a similar energy. This would explain why if you really exam the sexual partners you've had, they are either repeat partners and/or partners that are similar in thinking, emotions, and spirituality.

IT'S WORTH THE WAIT

During your time of singleness, I encourage you to refrain from sex. It may be difficult but it is possible. Sex is more than just an act. Sex connects you to a whole population of different people and different diseases. A *disease* is defined as a particular abnormal condition, a disorder of a structure or function, that affects part or all of an organism. This is what happens to you when you encounter a *spiritually transmitted disease*. It causes disorders in the way you function, and puts you in an abnormal state, and affects every part of you. Diseases create an uneasy way of living. Thus, the term *dis-ease*. Anything that attacks you to the point where you are dysfunctional or uneasy is a disease.

Spiritual transmitted diseases destroy everything that you hoped to build with your singleness and journey to becoming all-one. You become socially dysfunctional when you are entangled by several soul ties. You don't operate at your best because you are carrying the theories, feelings, and contradictions of all the people you are now connected to. It becomes extremely difficult to hear your own thoughts, feelings, and desires because you are crowded with the yells of invisible people on the inside of you.

For this cause, it is wise to save yourself for marriage. This way when the two of you have sex you are only connecting with their soul and their soul is only connecting with yours. Sex handled this way defeats the transfer of multiple energies from multiple people. Also, it defeats the comparison that can occur when the two of you have sex. Often, the reason sex is interfered and isn't as enjoyable for married couples is because they have too many experiences to compare their partner to. This makes things very uneasy. That's the effects of spiritually transmitted diseases. So, the best advice would be to save sex for marriage.

THE CHOICE NOT TO WAIT

What about if you choose not to wait until marriage? Well, if you choose to not wait until marriage to have sex, I want you to first understand that choice is completely yours to make. No one can sway your decision, neither make you feel guilty. You are not a whore. You are not loose. You are the manager of your body, and you decide who and who doesn't get to experience sex with you. I don't want you to get caught up in the reputation titles that comes with sex; I rather you focus your attention on the diseases that come with sex. Both sexually and spiritually.

Whenever you make the choice to have sex, the question shouldn't *only* be how will they see me afterwards? But it should also be how will you see yourself afterwards. How will you feel afterwards? How will you be mentally afterwards? What energies of this person will you be adopting? Who and how many will be joining this sexual intercourse? Not because you are physically having an orgy; but because whoever they slept with before, you are about to spiritually share their experiences.

What must be determined whenever you decide to have sex with a person is are they (and their previous partners) worth being connected to mentally, emotionally, and spiritually.

WAITING IS HARD

Finally, let's say that you decide to not have sex, but are still struggling with sexual urges. First, I will say go to the father in prayer. He is the one that made us with sexual desires and he is more than willing and able to help us with having control when it comes to sex. The scripture reads "the spirit is willing but the flesh is weak". So, our father understands that while you are willing to refrain from sex, there are moments that your body will scream for it. I know people that have been successfully celibate for years. Not because it was easy, but because they rely on the father to be their strength.

And to those who aren't as spiritual or who have sought after the father and still are struggling to you my answer is simple. Ride this this out solo. Yes, masturbation. This is not a choice that is promoted often. And while many cover their ears when they hear the word. It is those same individuals that engage in the act in private.

I want to pull the curtain back on the subject of masturbation. Masturbation is self-pleasure. And is the only safe route to take if you don't want to be entangled in any soul ties, sexual diseases, or unplanned pregnancies. Masturbation relieves you of the sexual tension you experience without the sexual repercussions.

Whatever road you travel down when it comes to sex, whether it be casual sex, celibacy, or masturbation; you have to be completely clear of the effects it will have on your well-being. Sex must be handled responsibly and carefully. Your life depends on it.

Chapter 11

Leave Me Alone; Until I'm Ready

"It is not good for man to be alone"-**God**

While God will often call you to the place of "alone", we have to understand that this is not where he intends for you to stay. Being alone is only meant to be the preparation place for the thing that God wants to do in your life. God only calls for us to be alone, so that he can speak to us, tutor us, instruct us, and reveal his plan for us, without distraction or interference.

Remember Adam was alone. But notice while Adam was alone, he spent time with God. He spoke to God about his purpose. He spoke to God about his strengths, and power. And it was in this alone time with God that Adam received his work, and/or the thing he was born to do.

Once Adam received wisdom from God on what he was to do with his life, he immediately began to walk in it. He began to operate in his life's purpose. Then, God noticed that Adam had gone from the place of being alone, to being "all-one." Adam was whole. He was secure. He was self-motivated. He was living the life God created him to live. Then, and only then, did God say "it is not good for man to be alone." Notice, it was God who made this declaration, not Adam. Adam was not lonely. He was not needy. Adam never asked God, to give him a wife. It was God who made Adam aware of the need for a wife.

Something powerful was taking place in this moment. This was the first time that God said that something he created was "*not good.*" So, what was it that was not good? Did God make a mistake? Did God forget something? Well, let's examine this moment.

When God created the first human, the scripture says that "he created he them; male and female, he created them." This scripture reveals that inside of Adam was Eve, his wife. God never does something half way. God always had a wife prepared for Adam. God locked her inside of him. Remember you attract what is in you. Same was true with Adam. And God did not release her from Adam, and present her to Adam, until Adam was ready to receive her.

God already knew that he had a spouse for Adam. But before he gave her to Adam, he had to make sure that Adam was prepared and capable of caring for a wife. It wasn't until Adam was operating in his purpose, and in relationship with God, that God presented him a wife. This was what God meant when he said that "it is not good for man to be alone." God was saying "this man knows his God. He knows his strengths, and power. He is walking in his dominion and authority. He is living his purpose". God was saying, "this type of person should not be alone." Adam was now ready to take on a partner.

Can You Handle Company?

Why is it good for you to know this? Because not everyone is ready to handle company. Not everyone can handle a spouse. Not everyone has grown to the place of being "all one." Have you taken your alone time to develop a relationship with your God? Have you learned your strengths, weaknesses, and all the things that make you unique? Have you discovered your purpose? Have you begun to operate inside your purpose? Have you learned to love you? Are you ready to devote to selflessness? Are you open to compromise and collaboration? These are the things that you have to be sure of before you are ready for the company of another.

Remember God said, Helpmeet. He never said initiator. The person God sends you will be the person that will help you, and compliment you. And while it is wonderful to have someone to come along and make us better; are you prepared to do the same for them? In order for a relationship to be successful it takes two individuals that are *willing to work together* to experience the best love, happiness, and romance imaginable.

Throughout this entire journey, we've worked toward your wholeness, solidarity, and singleness. We've shattered the myth that because you are single it automatically means that you are lonely. We've developed your standards. Defeated your bad habits. Polished your values. Exposed your purpose. Studied the art of love. Progressed from a place of alone to becoming all-one. And we've taken some other courses of study in between.

What was it all for? To get you ready for this moment of promotion. To get you to the same place that our forefather Adam was. A place where you are now qualified to no longer be alone. A place where you can handle entering into a relationship or partnership with another. It is vital to reach this point on the "me" level before you advance to the "we" level. Many try to bypass certain development processes during the "me" level and jump right to the "we" stage. And they end up in a cycle of attracting and getting involved with people that damage them, or whom they damage.

The most unrecognized and unacknowledged veracity of dating or getting into a relationship before you are ready is that you are dangerous in this state. You could be a predator or you could be the prey. A predator to someone else when you have not worked out your issues. And a prey for another for that same reason. You might find yourself cheating, abusing, betraying, belittling, and committing to other hurtful things towards someone who didn't deserve it. Yet, on the flip side, you could suffer the same mistreatment and torture by entering into a relationship when you are not fully prepared.

Best to Remain Alone

When you aren't ready to go into the "we" level, you'll find yourself confused and frustrated with the challenges of relationships and partnerships because you still have some "me" level understandings to realize. If you have trouble with addition, geometry will be like a maze of headaches. And a maze of headaches and heartaches is exactly what you'll find yourself in when you try to advance to "we" before you comprehend "me". Struggles with insecurity, jealousy, possession issues, and other toxic behaviors are flashing signs that it is best for you to remain alone. A person with these types of habits only end up hurting someone because they are still hurting in some way. On the contrary, a person that is willing to settle for these behaviors from someone is self-inflicting and hurt as well. This person is one who should also remain alone.

It Is Not Good For You To be Alone

When do you get the green light to take on a partner? For everyone this answer varies. There is no timeframe. Date. Or defining moment where one can say that you are ready to enter a relationship or partnership. What I will say is before you take on a helper in life, make sure that there is something to help with. Get busy living in your purpose. Make sure that you have something to bring to the table. Make sure that you are responsible and accountable enough to enjoy life with another. Lastly, be clear on who you are and what you are looking for in a partner.

Once you reach this place in your life, congratulations, because you are now qualified to be a benefit and accept the benefits of another. And it is not good for you to be alone. It is better for you be in relationship with someone else. Sure, you are great as an individual; but you would be awesome as a couple. The world needs more couples that are whole, secure, and genuinely happy.

Living Single

While you are qualified to have a partner, you might not want one. You might be having too much fun *living single*. And that is wonderful. Let no one rush you into a relationship. This is not a "guide to getting in a relationship" book. This book was intended to bring you into a place of wholeness and self-fulfillment. This book was composed to introduce you to your best self; and assist you in gaining closeness with your Creator. As long as this was accomplished, this book has served its purpose.

LIVE SINGLE. LIVE BIG. LIVE WELL. WHATEVER WAY YOU CHOOSE TO LIVE, JUST LIVE!

TOO MANY PEOPLE ARE EXISTING.

www.ingramcontent.com/pod-product-compliance
Lightning Source LLC
Chambersburg PA
CBHW032045150426
43194CB00006B/427